PUBL
FIRST IN 190
IN DETROIT

PERSONAL AND HISTORICAL SKETCHES AND FACIAL HISTORY

OF AND BY MEMBERS
OF THE

SEVENTH REGIMENT

MICHIGAN VOLUNTEER CAVALRY

1862-1865

COMPILED BY
WILLIAM O. LEE
Late Q. M. Sergeant Co. "M"

PUBLISHED BY
7TH MICHIGAN CAVALRY ASSOCIATION
DETROIT, MICH.

Facsimile Reprint by Detroit Book Press
1990

To the Living Members of the Seventh Michigan Cavalry, and to their Wives and Children; and to the Wives, Children, Brothers and Sisters of the Dead of the Seventh Michigan Cavalry, who, by their Loyalty to their Country gave up their Lives that it might Live; and to the Heirs of those who have Answered the Last Bugle Call since Appomattox, I have Cheerfully Given My Service in the Compiling of this Interesting Work. Many Thanks to the Living Members of the Seventh for the Material that has been so Generously Contributed for it; to them all I very gladly Dedicate this Book.

WILLIAM O. LEE.

Detroit Book Press

Reprint by the Detroit Book Press
℅ John K. King Books
901 W. Lafayette Blvd.
Detroit, Michigan 48226 USA

ISBN 0-914905-50-3

Library of Congress Catalog Number 89-083404

OFFICERS

OF THE
Seventh Michigan Cavalry Association
1901 and 1902.

President, William O. Lee,
 379 Hancock Ave. East, or 99-103 Abbott Street, Detroit.

Secretary and Treasurer, B. Griffin,
 Carrollton, Saginaw Co., Mich.

VICE-PRESIDENTS.

Co. A, J. K. Fisher, Sonoma, Calhoun Co.,
 B, D. L. Gould, Adrian,
 C, J. N. Wilson, Auburn, Indiana,
 D, Al. Shotwell, Dimondale, Ingham Co.
 E, Walden W. Raymond, Williamston,
 F, C. H. Beardslee, Marcellus,
 G, W. H. Hibbard, Detroit,
 H, Ed. Bissell, Hickory Corners,
 I, Wm. Hastings, Albion,
 K, J. L. Young, Prairieville,
 L, W. Stringham, Augusta,
 M, Thomas C. Williams, Hastings,

EXECUTIVE COMMITTEE.

Geo. W. Hill,	76 Piquette Ave.,	Detroit, Mich.
Wm. H. Fisher,	1046 Warren Ave. W.	" "
Roswell H. Holmes,	23 Joy St.,	" "
W. H. Hibbard,	361 Cass Ave.,	" "
Jos. Doherty,	208 Fischer Ave.	" "

PREFACE

To the members of the Seventh Michigan Cavalry and the public, in conceiving, developing and bringing out this Personal Facial History, it has not been the aim or intention of the compiler to give to the public a wonderful work, but to place on record some unwritten history of the great War of the Rebellion as enacted and seen by individuals by incorporating their personal experience and observation as soldiers on the march or on the field of battle as they saw them, that such unwritten history may be recorded and placed on the tablet of history that it may be preserved to continue through the ages of time for the benefit and information of future generations. Two or more may write upon the same event transpiring on the same day and even at about the same time, and each description may materially differ, still you must bear in mind that each occupied different positions, saw with different eyes and that each has a different way and method of describing the event, still I am confident that each has been absolutely honest in his views and that events transpired as described.

The object of the portraits is that the posterity that follows may see the likeness of those who in their country's peril, jeopardized their lives that it might live for ages to come and to familiarize the readers with those who have contributed to this work, not only as they looked when they were young men, defending their flag and country, but as they appear as honored citizens and men of matured years; while their Personal's are a true record of them not only as soldiers associated with one of the best Cavalry Regiments and Brigades in that great War, but also to leave a fitting and condensed biography and record of them as honored American citizens and to commemorate their memory forever.

INTRODUCTORY.

THE MICHIGAN CAVALRY BRIGADE.
(Custer's Cavalry.)

No person or persons can write a history or even a partial sketch of the Seventh Michigan Cavalry without incorporating more or less history of each of the other Regiments that constituted the Michigan Brigade of Cavalry. It was organized and will ever be known in history as a Brigade, still it was more like a large Regiment. Almost invariably where one Regiment was, the balance of them were in the immediate vicinity; if one Regiment or more were on the skirmish line, or in a skirmish or battle, the balance of the Brigade was there as reserve to do and did their part when called upon.

In compiling this Personal Facial History of the Seventh Michigan Cavalry it has not been the desire, aim, or intention to slight or forget the part the other Regiments of the Brigade took, but to simply incorporate the faces of some of the members of the old Seventh in bold relief and get an expression of personal experience in camp, on the march, or on the field of battle, allowing the members of all other Regiments full credit and recognition when circumstances develop and incidents warrant as is very often exemplified in the sketches herein.

This famous Brigade of Cavalry was organized December 12th, 1862, and was eventually composed of the First, Fifth, Sixth and Seventh Michigan Volunteer Cavalry Regiments. The First was organized at Detroit in August, 1861, leaving the State for the front September 29th, 1861, with 1,144 officers and enlisted men, but before the final mustering out of its organization at Salt Lake City, Utah Territory, in February, 1866, it mustered into its ranks a total of 3,244 men.

The Fifth was organized at Detroit in August, 1862, leaving the State December 4th, 1862, with 1,144 officers and men, but before the final mustering out of its organization in 1865 it mustered into its ranks a total of 1,998 men.

The Sixth was organized at Grand Rapids in October, 1862, leaving the State December 10th, 1862, with 1,229 officers and men, but before the final mustering out of its organization in 1865 it had mustered into its ranks a total of 1,624 men.

The Seventh was organized at Grand Rapids in December, 1862, leaving the State February 22nd, 1863, as a Regiment of ten Companies, with 916 officers and men; while on July 8th, 1863, two more Companies, "L" and "M," were added to it, composed of 178 officers and men, making it a full Regiment of twelve Companies, with 1,094 officers and men, but before its final muster out as an organization at Fort Leavenworth, Kansas, in December, 1865, it had mustered into its ranks 1,779 men.

As fast as the last three Regiments reached Washington and the front they were assigned to the Michigan Brigade, which was commanded by Brigadier General Copeland until June 29th, 1863, when he was succeeded by Brigadier General George A. Custer while the command was marching through Maryland on its way to a point which culminated in the Battle of Gettysburg.

During that three days' fight this Brigade was continually on active duty, and the last day of the three days' fight was in one of the hardest Cavalry fights of the War, in opposing General J. E. B. Stuart's division of Cavalry commanded by Generals Wade Hampton and Fitzhugh Lee, the Seventh meeting them and crossing sabres in deadly combat, in which charge the Seventh sustained heavy losses, but with the assistance and support of the balance of the Brigade, more especially the First Michigan, the Rebels were driven back and victory won at great loss. The records show that this Brigade sustained the heaviest loss of any Cavalry Brigade in that three days' battle, as its losses were in killed, wounded and missing, 229 officers and men, and of this number the Seventh lost an even 100.

During their term of service the four Regiments that constituted this Brigade, which, after the Battle of Gettysburg, was known as "Custer's Michigan Brigade," sustained losses as per records at the War Department in Washington, as follows:

	KILLED AND DIED OF WOUNDS.			DIED OF DISEASE AND SICKNESS.			
Regiments.	Officers.	En. Men.	Total.	Officers.	En. Men.	Total.	Gd. Total.
First	14	150	164	6	244	250	414
Fifth	6	135	141	3	222	225	366
Sixth	7	128	135	..	251	251	386
Seventh	4	84	88	3	258	261	349
Grand Totals.	31	497	528	12	975	987	1515

While the Seventh did not lose as many officers and men as any one of the other Regiments of the Brigade, still when taking into consideration the date of their going to the front and their term of service and number of men in the field, they must be granted honors as determined and brave soldiers, the equal of any other Regiment of the Brigade, more especially when their record of losses by capture is farther compared with losses sustained by the other Regiments in Southern Prisons, which is as follows:

    The First Michigan 56
    The Fifth Michigan 76
    The Sixth Michigan 98
    The Seventh Michigan 83*
     * 53 of whom died at Andersonville.

Michigan, with a population of less than 750,000 inhabitants in 1860, furnished during the War the magnificent quota of 90,048 men as soldiers to help crush that stupendous Rebellion, or over 12 per cent. of her entire population of men, women and children. The records of her enlisted men show that they were good soldiers, faithful and true, and who served their State and Country well; still the War records show, and it is officially admitted, that the Custer Michigan Brigade of Cavalry sustained the highest percentage of loss of killed of any *mounted* Brigade in the service in the War of the Rebellion, where its record of killed was a total of 528 men. The Seventh Michigan Cavalry shows a percentage of killed and also a percentage of killed, wounded and missing the equal of any Cavalry Regiment in that war.

Men of the Seventh, you should be proud of your record; and should be proud that you were members of so glorious a Regiment and Brigade, and your children and their children and the posterity that follows them, will always be proud of the record of the Seventh Michigan Cavalry and the Michigan Brigade.

COMPILER

Battles.   Men Killed in Action

#	Battle	Date	KIA
1	Hanover, Va.	June 30, 1863	None reported.
*2	Gettysburg, Pa.	July 3, 1863	29
3	Hagerstown, Md.	July 6, 1863	5
4	Boonsboro, Md.	July 9, 1863	1
5	Falling Waters, Md.	July 14, 1863	3
6	Culpeper, C. H., Va.	September 14, 1863	} 2
7	Robinson, River, Va.	October 8, 1863	
8	Brandy Station, Va.	October 11, 1863	1
9	Buckland Mills, Va.	October 19, 1863	6
10	Richmond, Va.	March 2, 1864	None reported.
11	Wilderness, Va.	May 6-7, 1864	None reported.
12	Yellow Tavern, Va.	May 10-11, 1864	9
13	Haws Shop, Va.	May 28, 1864	2
14	Coal Harbor, Va.	May 30, 1864	4
15	Trevilian's Station, Va.	June 11-12, 1864	3
16	Front Royal, Va.	August 16, 1864	None reported.
17	Winchester, Va.	September 19, 1864	8
18	Whites Ford, Rapid River, Va.	September 23, 1864	2
19	Woodstock, Va.	October 9, 1864	None reported.
20	Cedar Creek, Va.	October 19, 1864	3
21	Five Forks, Va.	Mar. 30-1, Apr. 1, 65	1
22	Duck Pond Mills, Va.	April 4, 1865	None reported.
23	Sailor's Creek, Va.	April 6, 1865	None reported.
24	Appomattox, C. H., Va.	April 8-9, 1865	None reported.
	Numerous small engagements		18
		Total,	97

*Men killed, wounded and missing, 100.

Co.	Men Mustered	Killed	Died Sickness Wounds	In Prison	Missing	TOTAL	Average Loss.
A	143	16	13	6	5	40	28 per ct.
B	141	9	9	7	6	31	22 "
C	142	7	4	12		23	16¼ "
D	146	14	16	8		38	26⅛ "
E	156	11	15	8	3	37	23⅝ "
F	145	13	16	7		36	24⅞ "
G	144	6	10	1	2	19	13¼ "
H	153	3	14	7	4	28	18⅜ "
I	171	2	16	4		22	12⅞ "
K	148	7	9	8		24	16¼ "
L	144	2	8	18		28	19½ "
M	146	7	8	8		23	15¾ "
Totals,	1779	97	138	94	20	349	$19\frac{1}{17}$ per ct.

CUSTER'S
MICHIGAN CAVALRY BRIGADE MONUMENT, GETTYSBURG, PA.

DESCRIPTION OF THE MONUMENT.

This Monument was erected by the grateful State of Michigan in honor of the Michigan Brigade of Cavalry and its fallen dead who sacrificed their lives on the battlefield of Gettysburg, three miles east of the village of Gettysburg, Pa., on the Rummell farm, where the Brigade did its hardest fighting and the Seventh lost an even one hundred officers and men.

The Monument complete from foundation to top is forty feet high, built upon a foundation eleven feet square. The principal shaft is fifteen feet high, composed of three bases, plinth, two pedestals and cap, the upper pedestal being four feet through at the top, on which rests four columns twelve feet high, representing the four Regiments that composed the Brigade, terminating in a capital representing horses' heads. Above the capital is a ledge five feet square upon which stands the form of a dismounted trooper, eight feet high. The whole presents tall and graceful proportions, and is composed of eighty tons of Barre and Hartwick granite.

On the face of the third base appears the name of the Brigade, Division and Corps, on the plinth the name of the Brigade.

On the lower pedestal is a bronze plate three by four feet, representing a Cavalry fight; upon the face of the cap above is carved a wreath of oak and laurel; upon the face of the second pedestal is a bronze medallion two feet across, showing the portrait of General George A. Custer, while on one of the polished sides appears the Corps badge and Michigan coat of arms.

Upon one of the polished sides of the lower pedestal appears the following inscription:

"The Michigan Cavalry Brigade organized Dec. 12th, 1862." "The fame of the whole is not greater than any one." This monument marks the field where the Michigan Cavalry Brigade, under its gallant leader, General Geo. A. Custer, rendered signal and distinguished service in assisting to defeat the further advance of a numerically superior force under the Confederate general, J. E. B. Stuart, who, in conjunction with Pickett's charge upon the center, attempted to turn the right flank of the Union army at that critical hour of conflict upon the afternoon of July 3rd, 1863. Field held from 8 a. m. until 7 p. m.

"But foremost in the fight you'll see,
Where'er the bravest dare to be,
The sabres of thy Cavalry,
Michigan, my Michigan."

ABRAHAM LINCOLN.

16th President of the U. S.

Son of Thomas and Nancy Hanks Lincoln, who were married in Washington County, Kentucky, June 12th, 1806; was born in Hardin, "Now Larue" County, Kentucky, February 12th, 1809. Family moved to Illinois in 1830. He was Captain the Black Hawk War, 1832; appointed Postmaster at New Salem, Illinois, in 1833; surveyor and elected to Legislature in 1834; second election to Legislature 1836; licensed to practice law in Illinois in 1837, and third election to Legislature 1838; fourth election to Legislature and Presidential Elector on William H. Harrison ticket, 1840. Married to Mary Todd, November 4th, 1842. His son, Robert Todd Lincoln, was born August 1st, 1843. Elected to Congress 1846. Delegate to National Convention, Philadelphia, 1848; assisted in forming Republican Party in 1856. Joint debate with Stephen A. Douglas and defeated for United States Senate 1858. Nominated and elected to the Presidency in 1860. Inaugurated March 4th, 1861. Issued Emancipation Proclamation in 1863. Re-elected to the Presidency 1864. Inaugurated for the second time as President of the United States March 4th, 1865. Assassinated by John Wilkes Booth April 14th, 1865, and died April 15th. Remains were interred at Springfield, Illinois, May 4th, 1865, where they now rest.

GENERAL ULYSSES S. GRANT.

18th President of the U. S.

Son of Jesse and Hannah Simpson Grant, born April 27th, 1822, at Mount Pleasant, Hamilton County, Ohio. Was named and christened Hyram Ulysses. Appointed to West Point, May, 1839, where by a mistake he was registered as Ulysses S. Grant. Graduated from West Point June, 1844, and appointed Brev. Second Lieutenant and assigned to Fourth U. S. Infantry; stationed at Jefferson Barracks, St. Louis, Missouri. Was with his command in Louisiana in 1846, and from there to Mexico with Generals Taylor and Scott through the Mexican War of 1846 and 1847. Breveted First Lieutenant September 8th, 1847. For bravery was commissioned Brev. Captain, April, 1848. Married Miss Julia Dent, of St. Louis, Mo., in August, 1848. Promoted to Captaincy at Vancouver, Washington Territory, 1852. Resigned his position and commission in the Army April 20th, 1854. Re-entered the Army April, 1861. Promoted to Colonel of the 21st Illinois Infantry, June, 1861, commission to date from May 17th, 1861, Promoted to Brigadier General August, 1861. Captured Fort Henry, February 6th, 1862; Fort Donelson, February 16th, 1862. Won the Battle of Shiloh, or Pittsburgh Landing, April 7th, 1862. Captured Vicksburg July 4th, 1863. Promoted to Major General July, 1863. Raised the siege of Chattanooga November 25th, 1863. Appointed Lieutenant General March 9th, 1864, and in command of all our military forces, taking personal command of the Army of the Potomac against General Lee. General Lee surrendered to him on April 9th, 1865, at Appomattox Court House, Va. In full command of the Army until elected President. Elected President in November, 1868, and again in November, 1872. Made a trip around the world in 1879 and 1880. Died July 23rd, 1885.

GENERAL PHILIP H. SHERIDAN,
Dead.

Born at Albany, N. Y., March 6th, 1831. Admitted to Military Academy from Ohio, July 1st, 1848; graduated June, 1853, ranking No. 34 in a class of 52. Was appointed Brevet Second Lieutenant, 1st Infantry, U. S. A., July 1st, 1853; Second Lieutenant, 4th Infantry, U. S. A., November 22d, 1854; First Lieutenant, 4th Infantry, U. S. A., March 1st, 1861; Captain, 13th Infantry, U. S. A., May 14th, 1861; Colonel, 2d Michigan Volunteer Cavalry, May 25th, 1862; Brigadier General of Volunteers, July 1st, 1862; Major General of Volunteers, December 31st, 1862; Brigadier General, U. S. A., September 20th, 1864; Major General, U. S. A., November 8th, 1864, for personal gallantry and military skill at the Battle of Cedar Creek, Va., October 19th, 1864; Lieutenant General, U. S. A., March 4th, 1869. Commander in Chief of U. S. Army in 1879. Died at Washington, D. C., August 5th, 1888.

MAJOR GENERAL HUGH JUDSON KILPATRICK.
Dead.

Born at Deckerstown, N. J., January 14th, 1836. Admitted to West Point from New Jersey in 1856; graduated and commissioned as follows: Second Lieutenant, May 6th, 1861, 1st Artillery, U. S. A.; Captain of 5th New York Volunteers, May 9th, 1861. Was wounded at Big Bethel, Va., June 10th. Recovering, he was appointed Lieutenant Colonel of the Second New York Cavalry and Colonel of the same in December, 1862. He took part with his Regiment in the campaign of the Army of the Potomac in 1862, and in the Stoneman Raid in the Spring of 1863, when he commanded a Brigade.

He was made Brigade General, June, 1863, and took command of the 3d Division of Cavalry Corps, Army of the Potomac, at Frederick, Md., and continued in command until ordered to report to General Sherman's army. February 25th to March

4th he made his famous raid with 5,000 Cavalry around General Lee's entire army. Soon after the raid in 1864 he went to the army of General W. T. Sherman and was wounded at the Battle of Resaca, Ga. He was in command of General Sherman's Cavalry in the operations around Atlanta, and the March to the Sea.

He was surprised by General Wade Hampton at Fayetteville, N. C., March 7th, 1865, and lost all his artillery. Here, it is said, he escaped on foot in very unconventional attire, but managed to rally a sufficient number of his men while the enemy were plundering his camp to successfully retake all his artillery, which he promptly turned on the retreating foe, thus making their discomfiture complete.

Breveted Brigadier General, March 13th, 1865, "for gallant and meritorious service at Fayetteville, N. C."

Breveted Major General, March 13th, 1865, "for gallant and meritorious service during the campaign in the Carolinas."

He was appointed United States Minister to the Republic of Chili, November, 1865, and recalled in 1868, and was again appointed to the same place in 1881. He died December 4th, 1881.

Major General Hugh Judson Kilpatrick was one of the most accomplished and enterprising of the many brilliant Cavalry officers developed during the Civil War.

GENERAL GEO. A. CUSTER,
Dead.

Born in Harrison County, Ohio, December 5th, 1839. Admitted to Military Academy from Ohio in 1857; graduated in 1861. Was appointed Second Lieutenant Second Cavalry, U. S. A., June 24th, 1861; transferred to 5th Cavalry, U. S. A., August 3d, 1861; First Lieutenant, 5th Cavalry, U. S. A., July 17th, 1862; breveted Major, July 3d, 1863, for gallant and meritorious service at Gettysburg; Captain 5th Cavalry U. S. A., May 8th, 1864; breveted Lieutenant Colonel May 11th, 1864, for gallant and meritorious service at Yellow Tavern, Va.; breveted Colonel, September 19th, 1864, for gallant and meritorious service at Winchester, Va.; breveted Brigadier General, March 13th, 1865, for gallant and meritorious service at Five Forks, Va.; breveted Major General March 13th, 1865, for gallant and meritorious service during the campaign ending with the surrender of Lee's army of Northern Virginia; Lieutenant Colonel, 7th Cavalry, U. S. A., July 28th, 1866. Killed June 25th, 1876, in battle with Indians at Little Big Horn, Montana Territory.

FIELD AND STAFF OFFICERS

OF THE

Seventh Michigan Cavalry
1862-1865

Col. Wm. D. Mann, 208 Fifth Ave., New York City
Col. A. C. Litchfield, Oakmont, Pennsylvania.
Col. Geo. G. Briggs, Grand Rapids, Mich.
Lieut. Col. Daniel H. Darling, Joliet, Ill.
Major Geo. K. Newcomb, Traverse City, Mich.
Major John S. Huston, Williamston, Mich.
Major Linus F. Warner, Almena, Kan.
Major Robert Sproul, Saginaw, E. S., Mich.
Major James L. Carpenter, Blissfield, Mich.
Adjutant Duane Doty, Pullman, Ill.
Adjutant Charles O. Pratt, Detroit, Mich.
Surgeon, Geo. R. Richards, Detroit, Mich.
Assistant Surgeon Marion A. Shafer, Grand Rapids, Mich.
Chaplain Charles P. Nash, Holly, Mich.
Quartermaster Farnham Lyon, Saginaw, E. S., Mich.
Quartermaster Daniel McNaughton, Grand Rapids, Mich.
Commissary James W. Bentley, Hastings, Mich.
Quartermaster Sergeant Wm. W. Brown, Stevensville, Mich.
Commissary Sergeant Henry DeGraff, Toledo, Ohio.
Hospital Steward, A. H. Weston, Grandville, Mich.
Sergeant Major, Wm. Jackson, Saginaw, E. S., Mich.

1863

Colonel W. D. Mann

1893

COLONEL W. D. MANN

WILLIAM D. MANN,

Colonel 7th Michigan Cavalry.

208 Fifth Ave., New York, N. Y.

Born at Sandusky, Ohio, September 27th, 1839; enlisted at Detroit, Mich., August 22d, 1861, as Captain in 1st Michigan Cavalry; promoted to Lieutenant Colonel, 5th Michigan Cavalry, at Detroit, Mich., August 14th, 1862, and Colonel 7th Michigan Cavalry, November 1st, 1862. Resigned March 1st, 1864, and honorably discharged.

ORGANIZATION OF THE SEVENTH MICHIGAN CAVALRY.

By Col. W. D. Mann.

It may be interesting to the veterans of the Seventh Michigan Cavalry to learn from me the peculiar circumstances which brought it about that I should have had the honor of commanding that notably gallant and efficient body of men. It will be recalled by you that the Regiment which became the Fifth Michigan Cavalry was originally enlisted and organized as the First U. S. Mounted Rifles, under an order obtained by me from the Secretary of War. At that time, as you know, I was a young man, not a resident of Michigan, although serving as Captain in the First Michigan Cavalry, which I had entered at its formation under Colonel Brodhead the year previous, I desired to secure influence with Governor Blair to induce him to allow me to recruit the Regiment in Michigan.

At that time Lieutenant-Colonel Copeland, of the First Michigan Cavalry, who had been an eminent judge on the Michigan bench and had resigned his judgeship to go to war, was in great favor with Governor Blair. I therefore requested Colonel Copeland to accept the Colonelcy of my new Regiment, though leaving its command and organization entirely to me. By this means I secured authority to go to Detroit and organize the Mounted Rifle Regiment and a Battery of Horse Artillery. In eight days from the time I arrived in Detroit I had mustered in both organizations, full to the last man allowed by law. Hard work and close attention to drills and discipline in a few weeks made a magnificent command of these men. In the meantime Colonel Copeland had remained in Washington, seeking to secure a Brigadiership (he never for one moment taking command of the Mounted Rifles Regiment).

About the time he was nominated for Brigadier, but before his confirmation, Governor Blair, having his headquarters at the old Michigan Exchange, sent for me and informed me that there were two Regiments in process of enlistment and organization at Grand Rapids, and that he had notified the Secretary of War that the Mounted Rifles Regiment would have to be known as the Fifth Michigan Cavalry and apply on the State's quota. He said that while one Regiment, the Sixth Cavalry, was full, the Seventh Regiment, he thought, was lagging, and that as I had been so successful in making a fine command of the Fifth, he would like to promote and appoint me Colonel of the Sixth. I told him I liked my Regiment, that they knew nobody but me as Commander, and that probably in a few days there would be a vacancy when I could become Colonel of that Regiment. He then said it was not only my success in getting the men together that had attracted his notice, but from his own observation and from what everyone said, the drilling and discipline of the Fifth Cavalry was such that he felt I was more competent than anybody else available to go to Grand Rapids and get those two Regiments into shape, and he appealed to me to waive my personal feeling and accept the Colonelcy of the Sixth. I may remark in passing that Major Freeman Norvell, the Senior Major of the Fifth Michigan Cavalry, was a very intimate friend of mine, of whom I was more than ordinarily fond. It occurred to me that if Copeland was soon made a Brigadier and I was made Colonel of the Sixth, Major Norvell would at once jump into the Colonelcy of the Fifth, which promotion would be very gratifying to me. I mentioned this to Governor Blair, and he promised me that he would appoint

Norvell Colonel of the Fifth if matters turned out as I suggested. I then accepted the Colonelcy of the Sixth.

The next day, when the news reached Grand Rapids of my appointment to the Sixth, a delegation, headed by Mr. Frank W. Kellogg, member of Congress from that district, having among its members the distinguished Judge Withey of the United States District Court of Michigan, and others, came post haste to Detroit to see the Governor and to protest against my appointment to the Sixth, and demanded the appointment of Mr. George Gray, a prominent lawyer of Grand Rapids, who was anxious to go to war. Governor Blair sent to the camp for me, and on my reaching his rooms at the Michigan Exchange, I found this delegation in a great state of agitation. They very bluntly and plainly said that Lieutenant-Colonel Mann might be a good sort of a fellow, possibly a good soldier and a competent commander, but he was not a Michigan man, nor a Grand Rapids man, and as they were raising the Regiment there and as the order for the Regiment had been obtained by Mr. Kellogg, M. C., they would not tolerate Colonel Mann's appointment to the Colonelcy of the Sixth. Mr. Kellogg appealed to me in the strongest terms, assuring me that I would get the cold shoulder on all sides if I went to Grand Rapids as Colonel of the Sixth, as Mr. Gray was a most popular man, and he, Kellogg, would be greatly pleased if I would accept the Colonelcy of the Seventh, thereby leaving the Governor at liberty to appoint Gray to the Sixth. Mr. Kellogg asserted that the Seventh Regiment then had one thousand men and that it would be filled in a few days. Some two hours were passed in discussion of the matter, the Governor all the time quietly maintaining that he wished Colonel Mann to organize those Cavalry Regiments at Grand Rapids and that he had appointed him Colonel of the Sixth, and that he would maintain that appointment unless he voluntarily relinquished it.

It had been one of my pet schemes in planning the First Mounted Rifles, or the Fifth Cavalry, to have a horse battery connected with it, and to have the men of the Regiment very lightly equipped and armed with repeating rifles, making them with the battery a great force for raidng. I expressed these views, and Mr. Kellogg suggested that the Governor should authorize another horse battery to be raised at Grand Rapids in connection with the Seventh Cavalry. He also suggested that Colonel Gray should not be mustered in until after I was, thus making me the ranking officer of the camp at Grand Rapids. Boy as I then was, somewhat diffident of my own ability and impreessed by the age, character and position of the men surrounding me,I, in what I sometimes thought afterwards was a foolish moment, assented to the arrangement and accepted the Colonelcy of the Seventh with the authority to raise a horse battery.

The delegation returned to Grand Rapids happy, and announced what they had accomplished. Grand Rapids was pleased, and when I arrived there with my commission as Colonel of the Seventh I was cordially received by the people and by the 237 men who, in batches and patches, formed the so-called Seventh Cavalry. In the meantime Copeland had been made a Brigadier, and Norvell, Colonel of the Fifth. Comrades, I now frankly say to you, "some of you having been present and among those 237," that when I learned the exact condition of the Seventh I passed a sleepless night, that, my first night, in Grand Rapids, and I saw plainly that in a day or two Colonel Gray would be mustered in as Colonel of the Sixth long before it would be possible for me to be mustered as Colonel of the Seventh. My first impulse was to throw up my commission and retire from the service. Somehow my ambition, tastes, nervous energy, or patriotism, whatever it may have been, would not allow this view to prevail. Still, I assure you, I was very downcast. However, the next day I determined to go to work, trusting to the same luck that had given me the Fifth Regiment so quickly to fill up the Seventh, determining to make it as good as the Fifth or Sixth, and if possible better.

Some of you know our struggles and efforts and remember them well. I went to Detroit and arranged with Captain Gunther to organize a German Horse Battery. I also hired at my own expense a brass band. I did all the work with the press I could, and made all the noise possible to get you boys together. Two great magnificent Regiments, the Fifth and Sixth, had just been picked from the youth of the State, which had been a good deal of a drain on its resources. Michigan was not as large in population as it is now, so I found men scarce, and it was not until February, 1863, that enough of you had been gathered to the flag of the Seventh to enable me to be mustered as Colonel.

During all of that time I served without pay and paid my own expenses. By the way, the Government has never paid me yet for that service and I presume never will. I forgave it, because I got reward enough in the splendid record that you, my boys, made when you were strong enough to take the field. To have commanded the Seventh Michigan Cavalry in that great campaign of '63, covering their memorable fight at Gettysburg, was such an honor that I forgot, and have ever forgotten and forgiven, the misrepresentations and the peculiar circumstances that brought to me the distinction of being your Colonel and Commander. There were plenty of good troops from Michigan, there were plenty of good troops from all parts of the Union. There were none better, there were none quite as good, none presenting quite as many examples of personal courage, of devotion to the cause, and loyalty to their Commander, as the Seventh Michigan Cavalry. That so many of you are alive at this day, and that I am permitted to meet with you from time to time and to receive from you so many expressions of kindly regard and the affection of comradeship, is a grand compensation for whatever disappointments I may at one time have suffered. Long life to all of you, and let our good fellowship continue while there are two members of the glorious Seventh left to meet together.

1864.   1880.

Colonel A. C. Litchfield,
Oakmont, Pa.

Born July 15th, 1835, at Hingham, Plymouth County, Mass.; enlisted at Georgetown, Ottawa County, Mich., August 14th, 1862, as Captain in Co. "B," 5th Michigan Cavalry; was promoted to Lieutenant Colonel, 7th Michigan Cavalry, November 14th, 1862; commissioned Colonel March 20th, 1864, and mustered as Colonel to date May 15th, 1865. Horse killed at Gettysburg, and falling on me severely jammed me, but not so as to prevent my continuing on duty with the Regiment. Was taken prisoner on Kilpatrick's Raid at Atlee Station on railroad, about seven miles from Richmond, March 1st, 1864, and was in close confinement with five other officers and four colored soldiers until July 15th, 1864. For the last six weeks of this time we were put on one-third of a prison ration; was then sent to Macon, Ga., from thence to Charleston, S. C., thence to Columbia, S. C., where for five and a half months we received no meat whatever; was paroled for exchange March 1st, 1865. Brevet Brigadier General United States Volunteers March 3d, 1865, for gallant and meritorious service. Mustered out as Lieutenant Colonel May 21st, 1865; mustered as Colonel May 22d, 1865, and mustered out as Colonel May 26th, 1865.

BATTLE NEAR RICHMOND, MARCH 1, 1864.
By Gen. A. C. Litchfield.

"The fight of our Regiment with the 1st and 2nd North Carolina Cavalry under command of General Wade Hampton on the Kilpatrick-Dahlgren Raid on Richmond:"

Not till the morning of the third day's march through rain and mud were we aware of the intended destination of General Kilpatrick and his four thousand picked men, of which force the 7th Michigan Cavalry numbered three hundred and twenty, having left for picket duty along the Rapidan River near Stevensburg all such men as were unfit for the march, and had barely sufficient in number to keep up our outposts.

About eleven o'clock of the morning of March 1st, 1864, Quartermaster Farnham Lyon, acting on General Kilpatrick's Staff, rode back to me and said, "Colonel, we are going into Richmond sure. We have with us a Captain who was in Richmond last week, who says there are no troops there and our only trouble will be with the fortifications manned only by Government Clerks and book-keepers." Of course all weariness left me at once and I looked forward with exultant hope to the hour when the final and successful rush should be made, which would make us masters of the situation and put Richmond at our disposal. "But there's many a slip between cup and lip," and slip did we, but not before putting up a stiff fight with General Wade Hampton and a superior force of the flower of the Rebel Cavalry. Our hopes were bright until after we had captured the outer picket lines and tested the strength of Richmond's fortifications and the valor of the men who defended them.

I should say it was between two and three o'clock p. m. when we passed the outer picket line by Brook's Turnpike and took up our position under the guns of the inner fortifications; our Regiment was in position along this pike, in the rear of the command and facing towards its right flank. My orders were to defend that flank and upon approach of the Rebel Cavalry to hold them in check and burn the bridge over which we had just passed. A short skirmish seemed to cause General Kilpatrick to decide that it was useless to attempt to force his way into the city, for as he passed on his way back he said to me, "They have too many of those d—d guns; they keep opening new ones on us all the time;" so we retreated across the Meadow bridge. The Rebels, emboldened by our movement to the rear, followed and kept up a sharp fire on us from the neighboring hilltops. About dark we went into camp near Atlees Station, where our first fight subsequently took place. As was too frequently the case with General Kilpatrick we went into camp for the night and unfortunately he did not put out a regular picket line, only picketed the roads with small picket reserves. My orders were, "Have your men make fires, get coffee, and make themselves comfortable and put a picket of ten men at the railroad crossing." This picket Wade Hampton's advance struck about nine o'clock that evening; shortly after one of the pickets reported to me that one of our horses had been shot and our pickets were exchanging shots with the enemy. Almost at the same time, I should judge about thirty Rebels opened fire into our camp from just outside, showing plainly that General Hampton had taken advantage of Kilpatrick's oversight and directed his force to flank our picket and reconnoitre our position. I presume they exceeded their orders by firing, for had they reported without firing Hampton could easily have captured our entire Regiment and many from other Regiments. Perhaps not more than one hundred shots were fired before they withdrew. When this firing began my headquarters were at a farm house just across the road. I immediately went into camp and found considerable confusion, as is always the case with the best of soldiers when suddenly awakened in the dark by a rapid fire right in their midst. This was the first sleep we had had of the sixty hours on a rough and cheerless march in mud and rain. The ceasing of hostilities on the part of the Rebels enabled me to restore order without difficulty. I then assembled the men along the road in front of camp and told them we had probably heard the last of it, as I judged we had been bushwhacked by the same men that had followed us out from Richmond in the afternoon, but if it should prove otherwise I told them we could hold our own against a superior force by firing from behind the trees and being careful not to get between the enemy and our camp fires, which were still bright enough to reveal our position distinctly. I then ordered Captain Sproul to deploy his Company and proceed through the woods on both sides of the road about eighty rods, halt and remain as a skirmish line till he heard from me. I also sent Lieutenant Ingersoll with 20 men across a cleared field in front of camp with the same orders that our flank might be protected. I then went to Colonel Sawyer's headquarters and reported what had happened and asked for instructions, intimating at the same time that I did not think we were properly picketed. Captain Hall, who was acting as Colonel Sawyer's Chief of Staff, said I could double the force at the railroad crossing if I saw fit. Ten men as a picket being more than enough, an increase would not help matters, but really make them worse; so, turning away, I said with some impatience, "I shall put a dismounted picket around my Regiment."

Returning to camp, I sent for Lieutenant Holmes, Acting Adjutant, that I might instruct him to establish such a picket, but before he reported Hampton opened with two guns and a dismounted force of his men attacked Captain Sproul and his men vigorously with a Rebel yell. I could hear Sproul politely request the Rebels to cease firing and make vigorous and sundry threats of immediate annihilation if they did not. Then he would hurrah and encourage his brave men to lick h—l out of the blank, blank Rebels, and so they would had the men guarding our flank been half as well commanded. Just at a critical moment they gave way and Sproul being flanked was compelled to give up his brave and determined fight and seek safety in retreat. Then "there was mounting in haste" and the Rebel yell, "Git, you —— Yankees." About this time Sergeant Mead came to me badly shot through the shoulder, and I sent him to the rear. The fire was then rapid on our flank, but had ceased, or nearly so, on our front, which revealed the gravity of our position. I turned to Orderly Morrow and taking his horse by the bridle told him to put for the rear. My horse had broken loose when the first shell passed over, which was not more than two feet above him. Meantime I had directed Sergeant Carver to find Colonel Sawyer and tell him distinctly that I could hold my men in check but a few moments longer. I then hastened across the road to get men to strengthen our flank, but was confronted by six or eight Rebels, who called out as I approached, "Don't shoot, we are Rebels." I determined not to shoot, knowing that if I could manage to pass them and get into the edge of the woods I could easily escape capture, but at the same time intending if suspected of being a "Yankee" to put on the best Southern tone I could command and encourage them to chase the Yankees until I could make good my escape. But "The best laid plans of mice and men oft gang aglee," for I still continued directly toward them, varying my course just enough to carry me past them. Ten feet beyond them in the dark fringe of the woods I could have mounted safely and effected my escape when I was challenged by a fellow who seemed to have concluded that I was a Yank, my nice little plan left me in a moment and, as if by intuition, my thoughts reverted to the astrakhan fur on my overcoat collar and cuffs as being what helped him to identify me as a stranger, otherwise it would have been impossible for the slate colored overcoats of the North Carolina Cavalry and our light blue to be told apart on that dark night. Discretion being the better part of valor, I gracefully surrendered and was proudly taken and introduced to General Hampton, and one of the most stubborn little fights our Regiment was ever in was over.

We had fought from twenty to thirty minutes in a drizzling rain, mixed with snow, against two Regiments of Cavalry under one of the bravest Southern Generals. If General Custer had commanded our noble Brigade he would have led us to a speedy and brilliant victory, but alas! instead thereof I was left with one small Regiment of three hundred and twenty men to fight it out all alone. General Kilpatrick was justly criticised for allowing Hampton with perhaps not over five hundred men to put him to rout with his four thousand as good men as ever drew sabre. But the defeat was invited when Kilpatrick gave orders for the men to build fires, and then go to sleep beside them, with them as lighthouses to direct the course of the enemy whom he knew to be pushing a vigorous pursuit, for I had received orders from him about noon of the same day to be ready to form a line of battle in the road at any moment as General Wade Hampton was pursuing us by a parallel road and was liable to attack our flank at almost any moment.

Years afterwards, when a reconstructed Hampton occupied a seat in the Senate of this glorious Union restored, I sent my card to him and we had a pleasant chat over the matter. Among other things Hampton said, "I had no idea of fighting that night, but the thing looked so pretty and inviting I thought I would give the boys some fun." I reminded him that had Custer been with us we would have made it lively for him, when he quickly replied, "He would have made it more than lively."

Two gallant soldiers deserve special mention; noisy but invincible Sproul and gallant Sergeant Carver, who, some time after the fight was over, not being able to find me, started back as though determined to reach me or die in the attempt, and would not heed the advice of comrades to turn back, but was reluctantly forced to do so when he ran into a squad of the enemy and drew their fire. I never saw the brave boy again alive. I was terribly shocked when in prison at Charleston, S. C., to read in the New York Times the account of his death in the Battle of Front Royal, Va., the following August, from which place I tenderly removed his sacred remains to the village church-yard of his native town. All honor to all the brave boys who so stoutly contended in battle with a largely superior force of the very flower of Southern Cavalry, commanded by one of the most famous leaders of modern times on that black and stormy night in snow and rain.

Our pickets should be mentioned as watchers who did faithful service and guarded their posts well. I spent that night with a poor sufferer from the Southland, who told me he was shot through the lower bowels by one of our pickets in their first attack.

1865. 1895.

Colonel Geo. G. Briggs,
Grand Rapids. Mich.

Born at Livonia, Wayne County, Mich., January 24th, 1838; enlisted at Battle Creek, Calhoun County, Mich., October 15th, 1862, as First Lieutenant in Co. "A," 7th Michigan Cavalry; was promoted to First Lieutenant and Adjutant, July 1st, 1863; to Captain, March 22d, 1864; to Major, May 19th, 1864; to Lieutenant Colonel, October 12th, 1864, and to Colonel, May 26th, 1865. Was taken prisoner at Buckland Mills October 19th, 1863; escaped from the enemy just before daylight on the morning of the 20th, joining the Union forces at Harper's Ferry; was five days within the enemy's lines; was wounded in left leg at Five Forks, Va., April 1st, 1865; was mustered out at Salt Lake City, Utah, December 4th, 1865, and honorably discharged.

BATTLE OF BRANDY STATION.
By Col. George G. Briggs.
Address at the annual reunion of the 7th, October 11th, 1901.

The event occurred on the 11th day of October, 1863.

The name, "Brandy Station," suggests refreshments and hospitality, but, upon the occasion referred to the hosts, in trying to make our stay permanent, violated the usages of war as understood by the Union Cavalry, and, as a result, the grand reception planned for our entertainment broke up in a row. Our friends, the Confederates, took to the woods, while the faces of our Michigan boys were flushed with the excitement of victory and the exhilarating effects of a new beverage which, in honor of the place, we then and there christened a "Brandy Smash."

The engagement at Brandy Station did not rise to the dignity of a great battle, but it is especially remembered by the survivors of the Michigan Cavalry Brigade from the fact that, at this place, the command found itself cut off and completely surrounded by a vastly superior force of the enemy's Infantry, Cavalry and Artillery; that in the face of such seemingly insurmountable obstacles the command cut its way through this cordon of foes by a charge that scattered the opposing forces in front and opened a passage of safety to our friends on the opposite side of the Rappahannock.

It is difficult for one "war relic" to interest other "war relics" in a narrative of army events that transpired nearly forty years ago. If the effort to do so is made, the date is about the only thing not in dispute. The event itself takes its color from personal experiences, and so the story varies according to the position occupied and the experiences of the individual factor. To illustrate: My memory of events preceding, leading up to and including Brandy Station, recalls a day of interminable length, filled with hard work and great anxiety, and unrelieved by any cheer or enthusiasm until that final charge, which opened a way to friends and safety for our weary troops. What recollections are brought to the mind of those who were present at this engagement, by the mention of its name, I cannot say, but I am quite sure no two would fully agree in a story of the day's trials and incidents.

Brandy Station was an event in the experience of the Michigan Cavalry Brigade resulting from the retirement of the Army of the Potomac from its position on the Rapidan River and, at the time, there were those who felt at liberty to severely criticise General Meade for the manner in which the retreat was conducted. One thing is certain: from the 8th of October, when the army commenced its retrograde movement, until the 11th, when the last of its forces had crossed the Rappahannock, he left his Cavalry unsupported to confront and hold in check the pursuing columns of the enemy, and it was due to the exercise of high soldierly qualities on the part of our troopers that very serious losses were not sustained.

The day that culminated with Brandy Station can be briefly described. Early on the morning of October 11th, 1863, the Brigade left the vicinity of James City and reached Culpeper without molestation by the enemy. From Culpeper, until the command reached Brandy Station, its rear guard was continuously and arduously employed in resisting the attacks of an enemy that appeared to grow bolder and more numerous every hour. The delicate and difficult duty of protecting the rear of the Brigade was performed by the 7th Michigan Cavalry, under the immediate command of Colonel W. D. Mann.

To unflinchingly face and hold in check the advancing enemy until the receding column of your comrades is out of sight; to then break to the rear a short distance and again face about to meet an on-coming and confident foe, is a duty that only brave and well disciplined troops can properly perform. Breaking to the rear only to repeatedly face about in a new position, which must be held as long as safety will permit, is one of the most trying services that a soldier is called upon to perform.

Several times during that long and trying day I conveyed the compliments of Colonel Mann to General Custer, reporting the Regiment hard pressed; that the enemy appeared to be increasing in number, and that assistance was needed. To these reports the same message was invariably returned, viz.: "Tell Colonel Mann he must continue to hold the enemy in check; when forced to retire to do so slowly."

For a time we had the companionship, as well as the moral and physical support, of two of Pennington's guns, but as the day wore on, and the situation grew more critical and threatening, these friends with a voice of thunder and a tongue of fire sought a place of greater safety in rejoining their companion pieces at the head of the Brigade.

It is but fair to say that at the time the Brigade arrived at Brandy Station its rear guard had been forced well in upon the main body of the command. The events of the next hour proved that our foes had forced us into the right position, as we were thus enabled to promptly join the charging column which drove the enemy from our front.

The situation just prior to this final charge is thus described in the following extract taken from General Custer's official report. He says:

"When it is remembered that my rear guard was hotly engaged with a superior force, a heavy column enveloping each flank, and my advance confronted by more than double my own number, the peril of my situation can be estimated."

As eye witnesses we can testify that this report no more than gives a simple statement of the facts.

It is only necessary to add that for us Brandy Station passed into history soon after the Brigade band struck up the inspiring air of "Yankee Doodle," and when, with flashing sabres, two thousand cheering men went forward in a determined rush for a foe that did not wait their coming, but who broke and fled from the field.

An incident that occurred at Brandy Station will illustrate the general character of the Michigan trooper. It will also serve to show his self possession and dry humor under very trying circumstances. Just before the final charge a shell from the enemy's battery on the right struck and killed a horse and threw its rider to the ground. Happening to be near the prostrate soldier I stopped to ascertain if the man was fatally injured, when, to my surprise, he jumped to his feet, looked at me an instant, and then exclaimed: "For God's sake, General, let's all re-enlist."

I laughingly assented to the proposition, at the same time telling my plucky "boy in blue" that if he ever expected to avail himself of the services of a Union mustering officer he better be making tracks in the direction taken by our then moving squadrons. He promptly acted upon the suggestion and I trust he is to-night a happy and prosperous citizen of this glorious Union which he fought to preserve.

I feel a pardonable pride in the incident just related, because it was upon this occasion, and the only time during my army life, that any one ever called me General. I have long since forgiven the mistake as, at the time it was made, every trooper in the command appeared to me to be entitled to the same rank that I had so unexpectedly received.

The salvation of the Michigan Cavalry Brigade from capture or destruction at Brandy Station was little less than a miracle. That it was saved for its subsequent career of brilliant services was due to its fighting qualities, its confidence in the leadership of the beloved Custer, and the failure of the enemy to take advantage of a great opportunity.

The day was well over when the last grasp of the enemy was shaken off. Soon after night set in, and without further molestation we reached and crossed the Rappahannock. Here the fires of a great army, comfortable in camp, met our view, and I said to myself:

"The Commander of all these Corps and Divisions of men must be indifferent to the fate of his Cavalry, otherwise it would not be left unsupported, as at Brandy Station, to contend with a numerically superior force of the enemy, composed of Infantry, Cavalry and Artillery, and which for a time threatened its capture or annihilation."

Exhausted nature sent us to our blankets and we slept that night with thankful hearts that one more day of our "three years, or during the war," was over.

In thus taking leave of the Command I bid it an affectionate good-night, and to you, its survivors, I extend the greeting of a cordial good morning.

THE FLAG OF TRUCE.

(From Burr's Life and Deeds of Gen. Grant, Page 761, Chapter 56.)

The night of the 8th of April, 1865, closed upon a day of hard work and exciting events. By a forced and rapid march, Sheridan's Cavalry, with Custer in the van, had placed itself in front of the retreating Confederate army, and by stubborn fighting until after dark had forced back upon the main body that portion of its advanced guard not captured. The night passed amid distant sounds of preparation for an early renewal of hostilities on the morrow and the hurried march of Ord's, Griffin's and Gibbon's Infantry to support the troopers, which had gone around the enemy.

The 7th Michigan Cavalry, well in advance, was, like the rest of the mounted men, held in readiness for instant service, and Colonel George G. Briggs, its gallant commander, here takes up the narrative of the surrender as he saw it;

"In open order of column by squadrons we stood to horse all night. The long hours were passed in silence, as neither lights nor fires were permitted. The deep shadows of the woods in which we were posted and the chilly air of early Spring that settled around and over us, were not calculated to inspire a sense of comfort or contentment; so amid the gloom we thought of the morrow and the chances of battle. The gray of morning was just giving place to the stronger light of full day when orders came to move forward at once. Only a short distance to the west, and almost directly in front of our former position, a line of the enemy's skirmishers was seen advancing. My command at once deployed and was soon hotly engaged. Under the steady and rapid firing of our 'Spencers' the advance of the enemy was checked, held for a time, and then forced slowly back.

"While the engagement was in progress I rode to the top of a slight eminence to the front and right of my line, and from this elevation I was enabled to see what I took to be the entire

Confederate army. It was going into position in a sort of valley with higher land upon either side. There seemed to be great confusion in their midst. Squads of men were running in various directions, and artillery, foot, and horse appeared badly mixed up in their effort to form a line of battle.

"The scene thus presented was alike startling and suggestive. Scattered over the plain and along the inner sides of the bordering elevation was the army of Lee, cut off from further retreat and hurrying its preparations for defence. Its advance seemed to have been suddenly arrested, and recoiling from danger in front, was moving in masses rather than by well-defined lines or column to different portions of the field.

"At this sight of the enemy, in apparent confusion and without the necessary formations to repel an attack, I instinctively took off my hat and waved it above my head in exultation over the discovery. Here was the opportunity for delivering a crushing and final blow to the war, and I exclaimed aloud, 'Oh, for Sheridan and his Cavalry now!'

"Turning to observe the progress of my own command, I saw to my left and rear, as if in answer to my wish, General Custer's approaching column. Knowing the General well, I rode with all speed to join him, and hurriedly informed him of what I had seen, and the splendid opportunity for a charge that at the moment presented itself.

"Turning to his staff, he gave, in his quick, nervous way, orders to have the command closed up and pushed forward with all possible haste. Away dashed the officers with these orders to his brigade commanders and at the same time he said to me:

" 'Show me the way.'

"Custer's command on this occasion presented a most striking and beautiful effect in color, as also in concentrated power for action. Following the General and his staff, and thrown to the morning breeze, floated not less than twenty-five rebel battle-flags captured from the enemy within ten days. These, with division, brigade, and regimental colors of the command, the red neckties of the men, and the blue and yellow of their uniforms, made a picture—as with flashing sabers they moved into view—at once thrilling and beautiful.

"By this time the rapidly advancing column had reached a point from which its approach could be seen by the enemy, and while preparations were being made to send forward a dismounted party to let down some fences, a battery of the enemy opened fire, but the shells passed over without damage.

"Custer, from a hasty glance of the enemy's position, evidently thought a better point of attack could be had by the flank and farther on. Therefore he changed direction and moved to the right—a movement that soon hid his forces from the enemy and carried them by a road or opening through a piece of woods.

"When I first met General Custer at the head of his division, I had said to him:

" 'General, if you charge the enemy I want to go in with you.' To which he replied, 'All right.'

"That he would soon strike a favorable point for such a charge I felt confident, and as he moved away I rode back to my regiment, which was still exchanging shots with the enemy.

"As my command was deployed and engaged, it could not be used to join a charge, which I felt certain would soon be made. I gave it in command of the next officer in rank, and rode rapidly away to join Custer. Before I reached him there suddenly emerged out of a piece of woods three or four horsemen, the leader of whom was waving a white object over his head. This was the famous flag of truce by which the desire of General Lee to surrender was FIRST communicated to the Union forces, and by me it was first seen.

"This flag, which terminated the Civil War, was a common towel, and is now in the possession of Mrs. Custer, having been presented to her gallant husband in recognition of his brilliant services, and also from the fact that to him it was first directed.

"Halting a moment to observe this approaching squad, I soon determined by the speed at which they were riding and the direction from which they came that their mission was one of importance. Satisfied, from my brief observation of this party and its movements that no trick for my capture was intended, I put spurs to my horse and dashed towards them, and was soon face to face with the approaching party. Drawing rein for a moment, as we neared each other, the leader hurriedly asked:

" 'Where is the General commanding? We have dispatches of importance.'

"Pointing in the direction, I said:

" 'General Custer is at the head of his column right over there.'

"Changing their course to the point indicated, away they dashed. From the rapid riding I had done, the jumping of fallen timbers as well as two or three fences, my saddle girth had become loosened, the cloth had slipped back, and I was about to lose it. Dismounting to adjust this difficulty, I was delayed a few minutes.

"In the meantime the party I had directed to General Custer had reached him, and by the time I came up they were starting to return with Custer's answer, General Whittaker, his chief-of-staff, accompanying them.

"Things were moving very rapidly then. What takes much time to write occupied very little time in fact. To arrest the further spilling of blood and prevent a collision of troops liable to occur at any moment, was the object of Lee, and this his messengers understood. They had ridden hard with a message intended to arrest the farther advance of the Union troops, and with equal speed did they return with the answer.

"From General Custer I obtained permission to accompany this returning party, but there was no opportunity for conversation with those composing it, for it was little less than a race, and one so hot that, with a horse already pretty well blown from hard riding, I was barely able to keep up. Indeed, on this occasion, and for the reason named, I might have been called a 'rear guard.' In explanation of my poor mount on this occasion, it may be well to say that during the seven preceding days I had lost three horses, killed in battle, and thus it happened that on the morning of the 9th my steed was not a thoroughbred. He was unequal to the work that day given him, and was never fit to ride again.

"Dismounting at Lee's headquarters, I was met by several officers who inquired:

" 'What's up?'

"Stopping to make reply, I soon became an object of interest and the center of quite a group of anxious and animated men, most of whom seemed unaware of what was then transpiring. When, in answer to an inquiry as to what the meaning of this flag of truce was, I answered, 'I think about your terms to surrender,' the proposition was promptly rejected.

"Numerous expressions of dissent were made, and one officer in particular was quite indignant—felt personally insulted and wanted satisfaction. He was at once suppressed, one of his brother officers saying to him:

" 'This officer is here under a flag of truce, is entitled to its protection, and you should not insult him.'

"Than the army of Lee none, I believe, was ever more loyal to its chief; and from the temper and disposition of his officers even on the day of surrender I am confident if he had directed they would have cheerfully gone into battle to the death.

"During the short time I was observing these things—say twenty minutes—officers were continually coming and going, and several prominent Generals were pointed out. Among such as I remember were Longstreet, Hill, and Gordon. While thus engaged, and having my attention directed to other matters I had not noticed the reappearance of my party until after it had mounted and was moving away. My 'Good day, gentlemen,' and military salute as mounting I rode away, were politely but not very cordially returned. I did not attempt to overtake the now rapid riding party returning to General Custer, but after following their course through the enemy's lines I changed direction and rode back to where I had left my regiment.

"Once there, I told the officers the story of my adventures, and we congratulated each other upon the prospect of a speedy termination of the war. The appearance of the flag of truce and the request of Lee were rapidly communicated to the army, and while it arrested all further fighting, no one knew whether those in consultation would agree or not; and so our forces were massed, and we again stood to horse awaiting results. All were nervous and excited. The final and official notice of the surrender was not received until about 3 p. m., if I remember aright, and then followed a scene that I can no more describe than I can forget. The tension of a mental strain, such as those who hourly face danger and death can only know, was suddenly loosened. Visions of home and loved ones appeared, and joy alone dimmed many an eye, and from lips the power of speech was often taken."

1863.   1901.

LIEUTENANT COLONEL DANIEL H. DARLING,
Joliet, Ill.

Born at Painesville, Lake County, Ohio, June 8th, 1836; enlisted at East Saginaw, Mich., August 1st, 1862, as private in the 7th Michigan Cavalry; promoted to Captain October 15th, 1862, of Co. "C," to Major, March 22d, 1864, and to Leieutenant Colonel, May 26th, 1865; not mustered as Lieutenant Colonel; was mustered out at Jackson, Mich., December 16th, 1865, and honorably discharged.

AN INCIDENT IN THE HISTORY OF THE 7TH MICHIGAN CAVALRY.

By Lieutenant Colonel Daniel H. Darling.

In the late summer and early fall of 1865 our regiment had its headquarters at Fort Halleck, at the base of Medicine Bow Mountain, on the eastern front of the Rocky range in Wyoming.

This post—now abandoned—was on the great trail from the States to Utah, Idaho, Montana, etc., and on an average 100 wagons per day passed loaded with Government or private freight.

One hot morning I was waited on by a small party from one of these trains which had camped over night near the Fort. The wagon-master, who was the spokesman of the party, informed me that one of the men belonging to his train had shot and killed another, and he wished me to hear the testimony in the case and decide what should be done with the man who did the shooting. To this I objected, telling him that I was not doing business in the judicial line at present, but the wagon-master insisted that as we were entirely outside the pale of civil law, the military was the only source they could appeal to for justice and protection. Moreover, in this case a man's life was in jeopardy, and that unless we took the matter in hand and settled it, the man himself would be murdered before another day began; that whatever our verdict might be, he would see that it was respected and carried out, for then he would be acting under authority. At this point the accused himself came forward to beg me to hear and settle the case. He was a tall, slim young fellow with light hair, and naturally a pleasing countenance, but at the time he wore a haggard and distressed aspect, so nervous and depressed that he could hardly speak, while his knees knocked together in his frightened weakness.

So I finally decided to hear the case and give him a trial. Adjutant Pratt was detailed as Clerk of the Court, and authorized to swear the witnesses. Witnesses were examined for the prosecution and defence, and what they said was carefully written down. Then the Court adjourned until afternoon to give the Judge time to review the testimony and write his verdict. At the appointed time he gave his decision, properly signed and sealed.

It was to the effect that the accused was acquitted, that the homicide was justifiable, and that the only criticism the Court had to make was, that the young man ought to have used his pistol sooner and shot three or four men instead of one.

The wagon-master accepted the verdict as all right and declared that if any man in the train attempted to further disturb the young man on account of this affair he would not hesitate to shoot him on the spot.

Later in the day I had an interview with the young man, and found that he had graduated from Yale College the previous June, and being in poor health and threatened with a pulmonary disease, his physician advised him to go West onto the "plains" and rough it for a while. Accordingly he went to Omaha and hired himself to drive three yoke of oxen and a load of freight through to Idaho in a train of one hundred wagons and one hundred men. This lot of "bull-whackers" was made up of old hands mostly, and many of them were ignorant and vicious.

They soon discovered that this young man was a thin-skinned tender-foot, and they took every means in their power to make his life miserable. By their behavior one would think they were related to the undergraduates at West Point. He had to gather the fuel to make the mess, do all the cooking, run for water, hunt for stray cattle, yoke their teams, etc., and if he did not move with sufficient agility to suit them, a pistol shot around his feet or an ox gad over his back would hurry him off. At length someone knocked him over with an ox bow and the "worm turned." He informed them that they must stop and let him alone or he would use his pistol. When one insolent unbeliever tried to bring him under again, he shot him, and then they clamored for his life. The wagon-master gave him temporary protection till they reached our Fort and had the matter settled.

Next morning the train moved on, and to make assurance doubly sure, I sent a small escort for a matter of fifty miles, but all seemed quiet and settled.

I had several letters and papers from the young man from San Francisco, Japan, and other points on his journey around the world, but finally lost track of him, and know not whether he be alive or dead.

His name was McGuffy, of Cincinnati, son of the author of the celebrated series of School Readers.

Not long after this event a young couple from somewhere came to the Fort to have me unite them in marriage, but I drew the line right here and positively refused.

Some of the officers took pity on them and tried to have the Quartermaster marry them, but he refused and someone else was vainly appealed to. Finally they took the pair to the blacksmith, and he welded them together, so I was told.

1863.

Major George K. Newcombe,
Traverse City, Mich.

Born at Westfield, Chautauqua County, N. Y., August 16th, 1833; enlisted at Owosso, Shiawassee County, Mich., October 12th, 1861, as Captain of Co. "F," 9th Michigan Infantry; was promoted to Major 7th Michigan Cavalry, December 10th, 1862; was wounded by rifle shot in leg at Gettysburg in Custer's famous mounted charge; mustered out at Owosso, Shiawassee County, Mich., October 12th, 1863, and honorably discharged.

1863.

MAJOR HENRY W. GRANGER,
"Dead."

Born April 4th, 1823, at Champion, Jefferson County, N. Y.; enlisted as First Lieutenant in New York Lincoln Cavalry, August 14th, 1861; was promoted to Major in the 7th Michigan Cavalry December 20th, 1862; killed in action at Yellow Tavern, Va., May 11th, 1864.

Major Granger was a heroic and brave officer, respected by his superiors and worshipped by his men. He had all the requisites of a magnificent officer, was cool in action, vigilant and bold, and was held in highest esteem by General George A. Custer. His death was regretted by every member of his Regiment, and in fact by the Brigade he was associated with.

1864. 1901.

Major Robert Sproul,
608 North Franklin St., Saginaw, Mich.

Born October 10th, 1836, at Cleveland, Ohio; enlisted at Birch Run, Saginaw County, Mich., August 15th, 1862, as private in Co. "C," 7th Michigan Cavalry; was promoted to Second Lieutenant November 13th, 1862, to Captain, June 23d, 1863, and to Major, May 24th, 1865; was wounded at Raccoon Ford, Va., September 16th, 1863, by shell in right arm, and at Fort Royal Gap, Va., August 16th, 1864, in arm by gunshot. Transferred to 1st Michigan Veteran Cavalry November 17th, 1865. Mustered out at Detroit, Mich., March 10th, 1866, and honorably discharged.

BATTLE OF TREVILIAN'S STATION, VA.
By Major Robert Sproul.

I would like to correct a statement in an article that I saw a few years ago to the effect that the 5th Michigan Cavalry opened the fight at the Battle of Trevilian's Station, June 11, 1864. The facts are these: The Rebels began charging the picket reserves of the 7th Michigan Cavalry about half-past three of that morning and soon after were repulsed by our men, and then the 5th Michigan Cavalry became engaged about one and a half miles away and near Trevilian's Station doing great work; they captured the Rebel wagon train, but did not stop there. We followed the 1st out as a flank, came up to the train and left our lead horses and Brigade H. Q. wagon with them. It was not long before the enemy came along and took the whole thing, including our lead horses, everything we had to eat, not even leaving the niggers, or a thing to cook with, in fact, cleaned everything out.

About this time the 7th was engaged in three different directions at once, charging right, left, and front in small detachments. While our men were making these charges the Rebels ran out one gun of a battery; our men immediately charged it, driving the Rebels off, but in turn they returned the charge and our boys were obliged to fall back without the gun. They rallied and made another charge and this time they were successful in capturing the gun and it remained with us. About the time this was going on my attention was directed to another part of the field, where I saw six of our men wheel into line and make a charge on a detachment of the enemy, who were coming out of the woods and about to make a charge on our right; they broke for the woods and did not bother us again from that quarter. After seeing this independent charge by our men I formed an opinion that just such work and under such circumstances is where the United States soldier is a better soldier than all others.

History has said but very little in regard to this Battle, but some day when a true and complete history has been written the Battle of Trevilian's Station will rank as one of the fiercest and hottest engagements the Michigan Brigade ever took part in.

1861.   1901.

Major Jas. L. Carpenter,

Blissfield, Mich.

Born April 11th, 1834, at Norfolk, St. Lawrence County, N. Y.; enlisted at Scipio, Hillsdale County, Mich., November 5th, 1862, as private in the 7th Michigan Cavalry; was promoted to First Lieutenant, Co. "F," October 15th, 1862, promoted to Captain June 8th, 1863, and promoted to Major March 26th, 1865; was wounded at Gettysburg July 3d, 1863, being shot entirely through the body on left side near the heart; transferred to 1st Michigan Veteran Cavalry November 17th, 1865, and mustered as Major to date from December 4th, 1865, by special direction of the Secretary of War, to amend record. On detached service at Denver, Col., as A. A. A. G., with

MY EXPERIENCE AT GETTYSBURG.

By Major James L. Carpenter.

At the Battle of Gettysburg we were in line company front, "A" first, "F" second.

About three p. m., July 3rd, 1863, we were ordered forward at trot until we came to a strong ridered worm fence, where we met a lot of Johnnies, and with our carbines and pistols we drove them from under the fence. Colonel Briggs (then Adjutant), George Lunday of Co. "F," and others jumped from their horses and made a gap wide enough for us to pass. Each Company had to break off by fours from the right into column. When Co. "F," led by Sergt. Buck, reached the gap in the fence we got a volley from the Rebel Cavalry at the right, which killed Buck's horse and wounded me, the ball passing through my left side. I felt as if some one had punched me hard with a stick, but did not fall from my horse. I saw blood on my shirt, moved my left arm and concluded that I was not dead, then touched my horse with spurs and she jumped through the opening and passed Buck's horse. My strength then gave out and breath became short, so I reined out of column and dismounted. As I did so a riderless horse jumped the fence and jammed me between him and my horse. I did not fall, but let my horse go and crawled back over the fence, there found one of our men with a prisoner who was about to get away from him. I drew my pistol and ordered prisoner to go on and he obeyed.

I was now tottering and looking for a safe place to lie down, when a gentlemanly Rebel asked me for my pistol. I gave it to him. He asked me if I was wounded and then said, "Hang on to my stirrup straps and come on." I went a few rods and fell to the ground, saw my captor watching me closely while he was trying to manipulate two single-barrel, large-hilted derringer; it was too much for him and I smiled at his awkwardness. He soon left me. Next I saw a column of Cavalry, four abreast, charging toward me at a gallop. I feared they would trample on me so rolled over out of their path and escaped injury as they whizzed by like a shot. While I lay there a soldier in blue came out of the thicket which was between me and our troops. He had a Burnside carbine. I told him I was wounded and asked him if I could crawl away. He undoubtedly thought I was a Rebel and for an answer dropped on one knee and took deliberate aim at me; I thought I could see down the gun barrel to the ball; the gun snapped; he rapped it on the side and again took aim as before; the gun again snapped; he got up, cursed the gun and went away. Shells from our side fell so near that when they burst the pieces striking the ground threw dirt on me.

I became unconscious and one of my men, Warren Wolcott, from the ambulance train, found me, rolled me over and thought me dead and so reported. Near dark I came to and heard two guns, one from each way along the fence, and heard the bullets sing as they passed. I thought best to go, but how? I could not move at first; but hearing Union songs in the distance decided to try to go to them; with the help of my steel scabbard which hung to my belt, I raised myself to a sitting posture, but my head whirled and I came near falling back again; perspiration started and I felt better. By raising my body on my right arm and hand and drawing up my legs I swung along a foot or so at a time till I passed around the thicket above mentioned, came to a fence, passed through a gap and rested under a small bushy tree.

While I lay there two men came near, calling for wounded and saying they wanted to care for them, but as I did not know which side they belonged to I lay low till they were gone. I then got up and walked some, but crawled more, till near the place where I heard the Union songs. They were preparing to leave, I called as loud as I could, they paid no attention; I called again, my strength and voice about gone, this time they heard me. They were a burial party and when convinced that I was a friend they put me on a mule. I thought the jarring of the mule would kill me and begged so that they took me off and laid me on the soft side of a pile of square timber. Soon an ambulance came for me, but the rolling motion caused great pain. After a long trip we stopped till morning, then Dr. Richards, Assistant Surgeon of our Regiment, came to see me and I was taken into a barn and placed on straw on the floor.

Dr. Richards was ordered away, but Dr. Sinclaire, of the 5th Cavalry, cared for me as well as circumstances would permit. He probed my wound and I fainted. My side was black and blue from hip to arm, caused by being crushed between the horses. That was my condition on the glorious 4th of July, 1863; I stayed there all day and all night.

Fortunately, Joel Harrison came to me that day and next morning he had me moved in a carriage into the City of Gettysburg. I was placed in a church where boards were spread on the top of the pews with only blankets on them to make the wounded comfortable. Poor George Lunday and I slept the night there. He had been wounded, the ball entered his head near the nose and passed near an artery, which a few days later sloughed through and he bled to death in fifteen minutes. A Lieutenant of the Fifth New York Cavalry lay by me in the church and we resolved to get more comfortable quarters if they could be procured, so I asked the first man that came to the door in the morning if he could not help us. Soon his wife and daughter came and we were taken to their home, placed in good beds and well cared for. A clean shirt from the "Christian Commission" added much to my comfort. This estimable family was named Longwell.

In a few days Captain Mann came and took me home to Michigan. On September 10th following I returned to my Regiment with my wound still open.

In 1889 I returned to Gettysburg to witness the unveiling of Michigan's monument. I there found Miss Longwell, the only survivor of her family. She showed me over the town, her old home, and the National Federal Cemetery. I there met a German who called to thank her for writing a letter to his family while he lay wounded and not able to write. He told her he still had the letter in a frame at home..

Miss Longwell told me she wrote letters for the soldiers all the time she could spare for weeks after the battle. She always carried writing material and a hassock with her. Coming to a soldier that wanted a letter written she would drop on the hassock, write the letter and pass on to the next. Truly this girl of sixteen was a ministering angel; God bless her.

THE BATTLE OF CEDAR CREEK, OCT. 19, 1864.

By Maj. James L. Carpenter.

Our Regiment was camped close on the right of the Infantry's extreme right post, facing south on the banks of Cedar Creek which crossed the pike between Middletown and Strasburg in Shenandoah County, Virginia. Although we were not absolutely in the engagement, we were near and around it and under fire several times during the day.

During the afternoon of the 18th, previous to the battle, we received orders to go on picket after supper, a detail of some one hundred or more men being made. We left camp, crossed the Creek, then by twos moved along a narrow farm road through low bluffs on the south side of the Creek. After going over the picket line and relieving the command then there, we concluded to set one more picket farther to the left after dark, which brought him well in front of the Infantry, they being on the other side of the Creek, so we gave them notice of the advanced picket. We ordered that no man hitch his horse when off duty, but to hold him; we had a fire well in the rear, as it was a bright and cold night. We were in a tight place if crowded hard; there was no place to back out save through the narrow road, we knowing nothing of the lay of the land to our right. About two o'clock on the morning of the 19th our picket on the left fired. On going to him he reported that the head of a column had appeared, and as his orders had been to fire on anything appearing from the front he had complied with them. The appearance of a column proved to be true, as it backed off, not answering the shot, fearing to stir up an engagement, which it did not wish just then, but went farther to our left to the Creek and by some means got in and attacked the Infantry's right post and also our Regimental reserve. They began firing on our pickets and pressing them in on the front, stirring up things generally. They were now squarely behind us and covered our retreat by the narrow road, so we were in a trap. We immediately gathered up our pickets, got in line, counted off and slipped away up the Creek, the Regiment crossing the Creek farther up to help us out. When I heard the clatter of horses coming up the ravine in front and on our right I dispatched Sergeant Buck to find out what it was. He discovered it was our Regiment and so reported, and then reported to Colonel Briggs that we were all right.

The enemy made this move, intending to drive in our pickets and perhaps bag most of the picket force and get up as much noise as they could so as to attract the Army to that point while they were quietly getting through the Infantry on the left to strike our men in camp, which they effectually did. The first order we received from Brigade Headquarters was to fall back and come around to the pike. The Rebels shelled us, which shots went over or fell short and hurt no one. When we reached the pike General Sheridan had just arrived at the end of his famous ride from Winchester. We saw him directing the movements of the Army and halting many stragglers. We crossed the pike and came into line on low ground and against a rail fence in close order so as to be covered as much as possible. Col. Briggs and myself were near together. Soon a shell from the enemy struck in a bank away to our left; it was a cross fire and we saw it coming end over end directly toward our heads. I have to acknowledge that I ducked down and I went down low; am not sure the Colonel did, but I should had I been where he was. The shell passed over us and struck a horse in the front rank, passing through his left shoulder, killing him, and through his rider's right leg, above the knee, from which wound he lost his life; he belonged to Co. G.

We soon moved around to the left of the Army. While moving we passed a horse that had been hit with a piece of shell in the top of the hip, blood was spurting from the wound, he still standing. I never heard such groans as were made by that poor beast before nor since.

We took our position full up to the front of the Army and a little to the left on a small hill for the purpose of watching any flank movement on the part of the enemy. We were to hold that position, and if the charge of the Cavalry was successful we were to move to the front. They gave us a shell now and then to keep us awake. This was the only engagement of the war in which I could sit and look on and see how the other fellows did it.

We saw the Cavalry form just to our right on low ground and begin the charge. They struck the enemy hard but were not successful, falling back to an open field, reformed, counted off, and charged a second time, when they went through, breaking the enemy up and ended the fighting in this battle.

We moved to the front, picking up prisoners from all sorts of hiding places. As we took one prisoner another near by called out, "John, have you surrendered?" "Yes," was the answer. "Wall, I reckon how as I may as well go, too." We moved on, still picking up men, till we had many more prisoners than we had men of our own.

It was growing dark when I discovered that our detachment was not attached to our Regiment or the Brigade. We soon came to Division Headquarters, when I reported our condition and inquired for our Regiment and Brigade. The Adjutant General told me he did not know much about it just then. He took my name and Regiment and told me to gather all the men of our Regiment that I could find and go into camp near by. He pointed out the direction to go, saying we might be wanted before morning, so you must be within call. There were perhaps a hundred of us in the detachment. We had not had breakfast, dinner or supper and we had had no sleep the night before and had been in the saddle all day. Our horses had had no feed, not even water, still there were thousands of men and horses in nearly or quite as bad a fix as we were. Amos Osborne, of Co. "F," told me he could get some hay for my horse as he knew where to find some. Being pretty hungry I called on him for his haversack, but there was nothing in it. After feeding our horses I went to foraging and found in my saddle pocket one lone quarter of a box of sardines, nothing more. It had been there for months as a reserve for just such an occasion. Osborne and I did not leave a scale, a bare bone or a drop of oil. It was now bedtime, but we had no blankets, so with the great earth beneath for a bed and the canopy of heaven over us for a blanket and the beautiful moon to light us we rested as though we were kings indeed.

About two o'clock on the morning of the 20th, "boots and saddles" sounded from Brigade Headquarters. We reported and moved down the pike to Strasburg and Fisher's Hill. The absconding Rebel Army had left the road full of army wagons, many hooked together by the wheels being locked, drivers probably having unhooked a horse from their team and pushed on. In the mad race of retreat they had left ambulances filled with the wounded and dead, big cannons jumped from the gun carriages, dead men, some with new blue clothes on and many other contraband of war were lying along the road. We were not accomplishing much, so countermarched, returning to about the same place we had left, and laid down. This time Osborne got blankets for us both. We got out in the morning and found the Regiment about ten o'clock the morning of the 20th.

My colored boy Jim had gotten back and found the Regiment. He came to me, saying, "Cap'n, I hurried back this morn'n 'cause I knew you was hungry, and I beat all them other fellows, but when I got here you wasn't here, and them other officers took all your grub." I told him that was all right, I should have done the same thing had I been in their place.

The lead horses came up soon and we breakfasted on hardtack, raw pork, etc.

On the morning of the battle the enemy got the advantage, drove us back and captured our Quartermaster and Commissary Headquarters; they found stacks of U. S. blue clothing and many donned them; they also found large quantities of whisky and downed it. On the battlefield many dead Rebels were found arrayed in blue clothes and many of our prisoners were well clothed in blue also.

So goes war. It was a hard experience, but we were not the only ones that suffered during that long civil strife.

1863. 1902.

Major Farnham Lyon,

Saginaw, Mich.

Born at Au Sable Chasm, Essex County, N. Y., November 5th, 1829; enlisted and mustered at Detroit, Mich., October 7th, 1862, as First Lieutenant and Regimental Quartermaster of 7th Michigan Cavalry; promoted to Captain and A. Q. M. May 24th, 1864; assigned to A. Q. M., Third Division of Cavalry, by General Custer, October 16th, 1864; promoted to Brevet Major and A. Q. M. March 13th, 1865; assigned Q. M. of Cavalry in Texas June 23rd, 1865; appointed Chief Q. M. Department of Texas December 8th, 1865; mustered out at Grand Rapids, Mich., April 17th, 1866, and honorably discharged.

APPOMATTOX.

By Major Farnham Lyon.

I went out with the Regiment from Grand Rapids to Washington, Washington to Fairfax C. H. I was not with the Regiment after we arrived in Virginia, but a short time before I was detailed on duty at Brigade Headquarters under General Copeland, and as I was vibrating between one place and another I did not see as much of the Regiment or become as well acquainted with you all as I would have wished. I had the honor of going with General Kilpatrick as Expedition Quartermaster on his celebrated raid to Richmond (not into Richmond). I continued with our Brigade on General Custer's Staff until President Lincoln saw fit to make me Captain and A. Q. M., when I left you on the James River and returned home waiting orders, and was assigned as Q. M. of General Custer's Third Division, Army of the Shenandoah, where I remained until Lee's surrender at Appomatox. Life here was very peaceful, with few exceptions while in the Valley, until the 19th of October, 1864. After that we were quite lively, as you all know. I happened to be the first officer from the front to meet General Sheridan on his famous ride that day, as we were getting to the rear as fast as mules could take us. We were about two miles out, and as I had charge of the trains he asked me what was going on, and ordered me to park the train right there. He left a part of his escort with me in charge of an officer, and ordered him to stop all soldiers and turn them back. The fact that Sheridan was returning caused very little trouble to get them to about face. Sheridan was right. We had retreated far enough. That morning will long be remembered. Captain Earl, Commissary, and I lost a good breakfast. As we were about ready for it the 19th Corps backed up on us and we were obliged to leave our red hot stove and breakfast for some Johnny.

It was my pleasure to be with you all at Appomattox Station on the evening of the 8th and the 9th of April, that memorable day of Lee's surrender, which has been so graphically described by General George A. Forsyth in his book, "Thrilling Days in Army Life." I was at the McLean House when General Lee arrived, and immediately after the signing of the papers by General Grant and General Lee I was ordered by General Sheridan to bring up the Cavalry Corps' subsistance train for the purpose of issuing Commissary stores to the Rebel Army. The order was as follows:

                      Head Qrs. Cavalry,
                      Appomatox C. H., Va.,
                          April 9th, 1865.

Capt. F. Lyon,
    A. Q. M. 3rd Cavy. Div.

Captain: The Maj. Genl. Com'dg. directs that you proceed at once to the Cavalry Supply Train in rear of 6th Corps Train, and bring it without delay by the shortest and most practicable route to this place.

The Trains contain Sub. Stores, which are required to issue to prisoners taken this day.

        Very resp.
           Your obt. Servt.,
                A. J. McGonnigle,
                  Capt. & A. C. Q. M.
                    M.M.D.

Head Qrs Cavalry
Appomattox C.H. Va
April 9th. 1865

Capt F. Lyon
A.Q.M. 3d Cav Div

Captain,

Genl. Smith directs that you may proceed at once to the Cavalry Supply Train in rear of 6th Corps Train and bring it without delay by the shortest & most practicable route, to this place. The Trains contain Sub Stores which are required to issue to prisoners taken this day.

Very Resp'y
Your obt Serv't
A. M. Ebright
Capt & A.A.A.M.M.S.

(COPY OF ORIGINAL ORDER)

67

The order as first received did not state the object of bringing up the train. On asking Captain McGonnigle where the train was, he said, "directly in the rear of the 6th Corps on the Pike." I said, "It will take me until midnight to get it here if I have to go around Lee's Army." He took back the order and wrote the above and said, "Ride a short distance from here and you will find a Rebel Major on duty, and when he reads this order he will pass you through the line." So he did and it proved a great treat for me to pass through the line of General Lee's Army that had obstructed our path so long.

The train was brought up and rations were issued to the prisoners that night. Early the next morning we were on the march to the South in search of Johnson's Army. The first chance I got that day while everything was fresh in my mind, I wrote a letter home, of which the following is a copy:

"Headquarters, 3rd Cavalry Div.,
Near Prospect Station, Va.
April 10, 1865.

Dear Father: Yesterday, April 9th, at Appomattox C. H., Virginia, will long be remembered by the soldiers of the Armies of Virginia. To say it was the happiest day of my life would not half express it. Language cannot express the feeling of the soldiers during the five hours of truce as we were in plain view, watching and talking with the enemy. The truce was to end at four p. m. All knew how it would end. Officers from either side found old acquaintances and had pleasant meetings. General Custer had a number of calls from old classmates. General Lee in going to meet General Grant passed close by, looking fine. At four p. m. it was made known that General Lee had surrendered the Army of Virginia to General Grant. Cheer after cheer was heard from the soldiers. We were ordered to move in the morning at 7 o'clock, and were feeling quite disappointed at not seeing the Confederate Army marched out, but I was not to be disappointed. About 4:30 p. m. I was ordered by General Sheridan to look up the Cavalry train and bring it up, and was informed that it was in the rear of the 6th Corps, which was directly opposite, in rear of the enemy. As supplies were to be issued to the prisoners I made the fact known to their picket, and I was allowed, with my Orderly, to pass through their camp. It was a grand sight for a Q. M. and thousands would have been glad to have been in my place for the time being. When about two miles inside the Rebel camp I met the prisoners captured from us. When they saw my red necktie, which General Custer and Staff always wore, one said, "There is one of Custer's Staff Officers," then such a shout as went up from 2,000 Union throats is not heard every day. I felt as good as they did. Everybody felt good. And all now think the last gun is fired by the Army of the Potomac, and as soon as the fact of Lee's surrender is known by other armies of the Confederacy I think they will follow his example. I am in hopes that twenty days will see the end of the war. Where we are going I do not know. We shall get supplies at Burke's Station, thirty miles from here, at the junction of South Side and Danville R. R. We may march from there to Richmond or go South, as the events of the next two or three days will determine.

I enclose a few sprigs, etc., taken from the room that the capitulation was made in.

General Custer has the little table the terms of surrender were signed on, and Colonel Whitaker of the Staff has the chair General Lee sat in when he signed it.

I enclose also a paper which I took off the table. I think it was used as a cover at the time.

With love to all, I am

    Affectionately yours,

        FARNHAM."

After a few days we learned of General Johnson's surrender to General Sherman. We returned to Washington and after the memorable review I left for Texas with General Custer, where I spent the winter.

If I had the time and did not impose upon you, I would very much like to touch upon the pleasant side of our camp life, for it had its pleasures as well as hardships and exposures. To me, as I look back, I feel that you of the "Old Seventh" were particularly kind to me, looking after my comfort when it should have been the duty of the Quartermaster to look after yours. I shall never forget your zeal and the many willing hands that brought up from "Morton's Ford" the old log house and put it up for my winter quarters at Stevensburgh. It was a perfect surprise and will always be remembered as one of the many kind acts bestowed upon me.

1893

Rev. Charles P. Nash,

Holly, Oakland Co., Mich.

Born March 16th, 1831, at Clarkston, Rockland County, N. Y.; enlisted September 6th, 1863, as Chaplain of the 7th Michigan Cavalry; mustered out at Fort Leavenworth, Kan., December 11th, 1865, and honorably discharged.

INCIDENTS.

By Rev. C. P. Nash.

I was with our Regiment in Kilpatrick's raid of February, 1864, Sheridan's Raid on to Richmond, May, 1864, and was at the front with the Regiment which participated in battles and skirmishes, viz.: Richmond, March 1st; Wildnerness, May 6th and 7th; Yellow Tavern, May 10th; Front Royal, August 16th; Winchester, September 19th; Woodstock, October 9th; Cedar Creek, October 19th. Never was captured or wounded.

I thought I was wounded once during the battle of Woodstock. Surprised while resting by Early's men, who had crept up near us under cover of growing corn, I felt the sting of a bullet whiz so close to my nose that I surely thought I had lost a portion of that important facial appendage. I instantly used my hand to ascertain how much was missing and was delighted to find it intact, not even the skin abraded.

At the battle of Cedar Creek, October 19th, 1864, during a lull in the storm of battle, I was requested by Colonel Briggs to go to the rear and toward the right of the line to reconnoitre. As I neared the main road I saw General Sheridan, on his spirited and foaming black, finish his celebrated ride from Winchester; saw a young officer an aide ride to meet him. The only words I heard were by the General, who inquired, "Where in h—l is General Wright?" I did not hear the answer, but I afterwards learned that that young officer was Major McKinley, our martyred President. It was on that same afternoon that while reconnoitreing, I got between the two lines of battle, and had to do what I supposed impossible, actually dodge cannon balls. I did not get back to report to Colonel Briggs.

1864   1901

LIEUTENANT DANIEL MCNAUGHTON,

331 South Lafayette St., Grand Rapids, Mich.

Born July 1st, 1837, at Moscow, Hillsdale County, Mich.; enlisted at Grand Rapids, Kent County, Mich., August 28th, 1862, as R. Q. M. Sergeant, 7th Michigan Cavalry; was promoted to First Lieutenant and R. Q. M. May 18th, 1864; was mustered out at Fort Leavenworth, Kansas, December 15th, 1865, and honorably discharged.

REMINISCENCES.

By Lieut. Dan'l McNaughton.

The late summer and early autumn of 1862 were indeed dark days for the Republic. McClellan with an army of 160,000 men—the best organized and finest equipped body of soldiers that had ever marshalled under the standard of any cause—had been outgeneraled and defeated before Richmond.

There was no pause in the victorious march of the Confederates. Swarming northward across the Potomac, they threatened the National Capital. In the West also, the situation was grave, and it looked indeed as if the God of our fathers had forsaken us and as if the doom of the Nation was sealed. It was in this darkest hour that the 5th, 6th, and 7th Regiments of Michigan Cavalry were recruited and hurried to the front in defence of the imperiled Republic. These regiments, together with the First, already in the field, composed the famous "Michigan Cavalry Brigade," an organization that at once became conspicuous for brilliant and heroic achievements. Bravely and well they carried the old Flag through the night of tempest and of storm, and returned it floating higher, and a new glory gleaming from its stars, its brightened folds radiant in the sunlight of a hundred victories. They shed unfading honors upon their State and gave to history the foremost name in all the annals of cavalry leadership in the person of the knightly and lamented Custer.

It was my privilege to follow the fortunes of the 7th Michigan Cavalry, and I have never had occasion to regret my association with that splendid body of men. The comradeship of those old days, the friendships formed and fostered in those far-off years are the most cherished recollections of my later life. I love to go back to those eventful times and linger along the pathway of those stirring scenes.

I touch the wand of memory and I am with the old boys again. I am with them on the dusty, wearisome march, and share with them again a soldier's couch, the covering being the clouds and the stars. I am with them again in camp and field, through mountain gap and over swollen rivers; I am with them at Gettysburg, with them in the sleepless watches along the Rapidan and the Rappahannock; I am with them through the tangled shadows of the Wilderness, with them before Petersburg; I am with them at Winchester, and follow again the banners of the victorious Sheridan as he sweeps like a cyclone through the Valley of the Shenandoah; I am with them at Appomattox, I am with them again in the gaily decorated avenues of the Capital City of the Nation, in that most magnificent pageant of modern times, where the battle-scarred victors of the Potomac and the conquering veterans of the March to the Sea met and passed in grand review before the uncovered heads of Courts and Cabinets—victorious legions of the most stupendous conflict in history passing through the gateway of peace amid a rain of flowers. I am with them, too, in that thirsty and treeless journey across the Western plains; with them in the shadows of the Rockies, with them in sunshine and cold.

I call old names and the old faces pass before me as in a dream. I see Colonel Mann, our first Commander, bluff, impatient and sometimes impulsive, but withal a brave, generous soul and a born leader of men.

Colonel Litchfield, tall and straight as an arrow, reserved and thoughtful, yet a kinder heart never beat than his. He was absolutely fearless and uncompromising in his loyalty to duty, and as soldier and as citizen he honored the State and the Nation.

Colonel Briggs, the ever cordial and courteous.

Major Sproule, who of the entire Regiment all know and love brave, blunt, generous, big-hearted, honest Bob Sproul. His language was not always such as is used in the Bible class, yet his presence was ever an inspiration and a cheer. There was no loneliness when Bob was around. He was the storm center of every innocent deviltry and the life of every camp fire.

Captain Lyon, our Quartermaster, a genial, jolly companion, a careful and conscientious officer, ever vigilant in looking after the comfort and welfare of the Regiment, a quality that has since made him the Prince of Landlords.

Another, Squire Wheeler, our Veterinary Surgeon, a quaint, comical Down East Yankee, and a great lover of fine horses. I never think of him without recalling an incident that occurred while the trains of the army were packed for a few days at White House Landing, Va., the summer of 1864. Wheeler was the owner of a beautiful chestnut, a large, thoroughbred, intelligent animal, one of the finest horses in the entire army. Above everything else on earth, Wheeler loved and prized that horse. A soldier by the name of Bingham was on detail at the Quartermaster's department acting as orderly, cook, or in any capacity where he was of service. He was somewhat of a granny, but a very honest and trusty man. His one great failing was an enormous appetite, especially for fine, ripe fruit. It was cherry time, and not far from the camp was an orchard of large cherries. That orchard set Bingham's mouth into an uncontrollable watering for cherries. How to get them was a poser—it was dangerous to go outside of camp on account of the many Rebels in the vicinity. Finally he prevailed upon a young Scotchman in camp, called "Sandy," to make a raid on that cherry orchard. "Sandy" insisted he must have a strong, fleet-footed mount for such an undertaking. Fitting "Sandy" out with bags for the fruit, and putting him astride of Wheeler's handsome thoroughbred, he sent the Scotchman forth on his mission. Wheeler soon missed his pet animal and accoutrements and the sky at once began to show signs of storms. Something was wrong and his old Yankee blood began to boil. "Sandy" and the horse never came back, as they were captured. Bingham's remarked uneasiness about them kind of gave the whole thing away on himself. Wheeler, even on ordinary occasions was never very choice or refined in his vocabulary, but the idea that he must be robbed of that valuable horse, the pride of his heart, the very apple of his eye, all because of Bingham's infernal appetite for cherries, fired the old man into such a frenzy of rage and profanity that none who heard him will ever forget. Even our good Chaplain, a very pronounced Universalist, at once changed his views in regard to a certain hot place, for he declared that nothing else but the genuine, old-fashioned, orthodox Hell could ever turn loose such fury in that wagon camp. Wheeler was captured a short times afterwards—horse, bag and baggage—and died ere the close of the war in a Rebel prison. Bingham, too, long since has gone to his reward. It is said that his last prayer on earth was an urgent appeal to be spared a meeting with Wheeler. I never learned the fate of poor "Sandy." If he lived to regain his freedom again, he never showed up with us.

There are other names upon my lips, and other forms and faces rise up before me out of the mist of years. I cannot mention them all, many of them are no longer among the living. There are Granger, Brewer, Mead, Carver, Corcoran, and scores of others just as noble and as brave, who fell in the forefront of the battle—gave up their young lives in the darkness of the struggle, ere they knew if the cause they loved would triumph or would fail. They reach to us the hands of loyal comradeship from the clear, upper sky, and many, oh! how many, have left us since the war has ended and answer our calls no more. We loved them all. They were our companions in arms on many a field, shoulder to shoulder they stood with us through many a trying hour. Holier to us than consecrated shrine or kingly dust are the memories of our soldier dead. It was from out their blood and sacrifice, their suffering and their toil that a newer and grander Liberty arose and swung open the dungeon door, where barbarism, wrong, lust and crime for centuries had chained the human soul, led out the panting and trembling victims that had been shackled and wronged, and they lifted up their amazed and wondering faces to God and thanked Him and them that they walked forth free men.

1883

LIEUTENANT HENRY DEGRAFF,
215 Ontario St., Toledo, Ohio.

Born at New Paltz, Ulster County, N. Y., December 8th, 1832; enlisted at Adrian, Lenawee County, Mich., December 4th, 1862, as private in Co. ——, 7th Michigan Cavalry; was promoted to Regimental Commissary Sergeant September, 1863, and to Second Lieutenant May 26th, 1865; not mustered; mustered out at Camp Collin, Colorado, November 7th, 1865,

RECOLLECTIONS.
By Lieutenant Henry DeGraff.

After the battle of Gettysburg, and after we had somewhat recovered from the sorrow and horror of the loss in killed and wounded of our dear comrades, in following up Lee in his retreat to Robinson River we had it easy—no fighting, no hurrying to and fro, and plenty of rations and time to eat them, and do a little foraging besides. We all know that a cavalry soldier always "forages" for something to eat; no matter how well stocked he is with regular army rations, he wants some "sweet-meats."

On the whole, I think at that time the Regiment was enjoying life quite well. I know I was, for one. I had plenty of "hardtack and speck, and sugar and coffee" to issue to the boys. Coffee and hardtack were the "staff of life" in the army; and in addition, and in place of foraging, I went into the sutler business for a short time. Joe Harrison—all headquarters knew Joe—he was a friend of Colonel Mann's—Joe went to Washington, bought goods, and I sold them and pocketed the money, and had a good time. Joe got his share, however, if I remember rightly.

We followed Lee up till he crossed Robinson River. About six miles before we reached the river, late one afternoon, we passed a mill-site, and Colonel Mann left me in charge, with ten men and a Sergeant, to hold it until further orders. Night was now upon us; pickets were posted, and we were alone to take care of ourselves. There was a grist mill, saw mill, woolen mill, and blacksmith shop, and one house. I pitched my tent in the dooryard of the house and was invited into the house by a very nice young lady to take a "snack," and also to occupy a room; the room I declined, with thanks, but the snack I accepted. It was fine, good soft bread and butter, cream for coffee, cake and preserves, and really I thought it a pretty nice spread. I enjoyed the evening, then returned to my tent and blanket. In the morning when I wakened a camp fire was burning before my tent, and the smell of chicken cooking interested me. I was soon washed and dressed, and took a stroll out to see what was going on. The grist mill, saw mill, woolen mill and blacksmith shop were all running full blast, and about five men in the cornfield husking corn for dear life. Well, I thought this was business enough for one man. Anyway, we had about two thousand bushels of wheat in the mill, ground it all into flour, used it mostly in our Regiment, gave some to the poor families. We stayed there about three weeks, then went to the front with the Regiment and stayed there a few days, when General Lee turned our flank and it was a race for Washington again. We were rear guard, and when we got back as far as Brandy Station—well, you all remember that little "fuss" I guess, I know I do—and all I got for that day's work was a can of peaches. At evening just before we crossed the Rappahannock I found a "lone sutler;" that can of peaches was all he had. I bought and ate it, and was satisfied. The next day, back from the river a few miles, I saw the Pontoon Corps of the Army of the Potomac corraled; it was a great sight.

Soldiers have a good deal of fun. I know I did in a quiet way. I often went on picket with Major Carpenter; always got honey—that is, "most always." Sometimes you got what you didn't want; but with Major Carpenter I always felt safe; would unsaddle, picket Jeff, my horse, and go to sleep. The Major will remember the morning we left Luray Valley and had to charge through the town and send on a flag of truce, as we were being fired upon by our own men. But I got two nice loaves of soft bread and some cherries, and got away, but it was a close call for me. They were "laying" for any Yank. Pretty girls, however, and were good entertainers.

At Luray I lost my best friend, Lieutenant Carver. We got across the river and found that Custer had five Johnnies hanging to the limbs of one tree, in retaliation for shooting a Lieutenant in command of our advance guard, after he had surrendered to Mosby and his men when in ambush, so in retaliation General Custer hung five, killed three of Mosby's men and held one prisoner.

1900.

Dr. Marion A. Shafer,
275 Lyon St., Grand Rapids, Mich.

Born at Yates, Orleans County, N. Y., August 3d, 1838; enlisted at Grand Rapids, Kent County, Mich., December 10th, 1862, as private in Co. "G," 7th Michigan Cavalry; was promoted to Hospital Steward January 24th, 1863, and to Assistant Surgeon May 28th, 1865, to rank as such from July 7th, 1863, by order of Governor Henry H. Crapo; mustered out at Fort Leavenworth, Kansas, November 7th, 1865, and honorably discharged.

AN INCIDENT AT THE BATTLE OF TREVILIAN'S STATION.
By Dr. Marion A. Shafer.

This sketch includes two persons besides myself, viz., Dr. George R. Richards, Surgeon of the Regiment, and Private Arsnoe—it being only one of the many hair-breadth escapes of the day.

At daybreak on the morning of the 11th of June, 1864, at Trevilian's Station on the Virginia Central Railroad, General Sheridan with two divisions of cavalry, Gregg and Torberto, confronted Generals Hampton and Fitzhugh Lee and two divisions of cavalry located near the Station. General Custer's Brigade, composed of the 1st, 5th, 6th and 7th Michigan Cavalry, was sent on a rapid march to reach the rear of the enemy's two divisions. General Custer, the moment he found himself in Hampton's rear, charged the lead horses, wagons, and caissons that he found there, getting hold of a vast number of each, and also the Station itself. In "Sheridan's Memoirs," Custer in his report says: "I was compelled to take up a position near the Station from which I could resist the attacks of the enemy which were now being made on my front, right, left, and rear."

Sheridan, in his Memoirs, states that Custer was attacked by Rosser's brigade on one side and Fitzhugh Lee's division on the other. There then ensued a desperate struggle for the possession of the captured property, resulting finally in its being taken by the enemy.

Notwithstanding the fact that Custer was fighting against great odds, he managed to take about five hundred prisoners.

About 8 o'clock a. m., Arsnoe, who carried the medicine chest, Dr. Richards and myself started for the captured train to investigate the ambulances for medicine or other supplies, especially for something to eat, as we had been cheated out of our breakfast and had nothing for dinner, unless we could find it. We soon arrived at the rear of the train which was standing in the road just as it had been halted that morning. As we rode along we investigated as well as we could, but found nothing but a medicine chest containing only a small bottle of the oil of Cajuput. We felt that we were on unsafe ground, so concluded to return to the Regiment through the fields. Arsnoe dismounted and let down the bars and we passed through. Being dismounted, Arsnoe had squatted down in the shade of the bar posts, as the day was getting warm. We told him to get on his horse, and an instant later the enemy dashed through yelling, "Surrender, you devils!" We heeded not their demand, though emphasized by a liberal amount of shooting, but put spurs to our horses, urging them on to their utmost speed, as the enemy was in hot pursuit. Dr. Richards had the lead and I was not far behind. Our course was over descending ground, and at the end of the descent some twenty rods ahead of us I could see a gulf, or dry creek bed, which lay directly across our path. If we could get over that I thought our chances for getting away were good. I could see Dr. Richards going straight for it. I sheered my horse so as to be a little distance below him, for I expected my horse to jump over, and if Dr. Richards failed I did not want to jump on to him. We made the jump all right and escaped, as the pursuers halted at the ditch.

Arsnoe was captured at the bars. If his first name was William, he died in Andersonville prison the following December. If it was Peter, he survived his imprisonment only a short time after the close of the war.

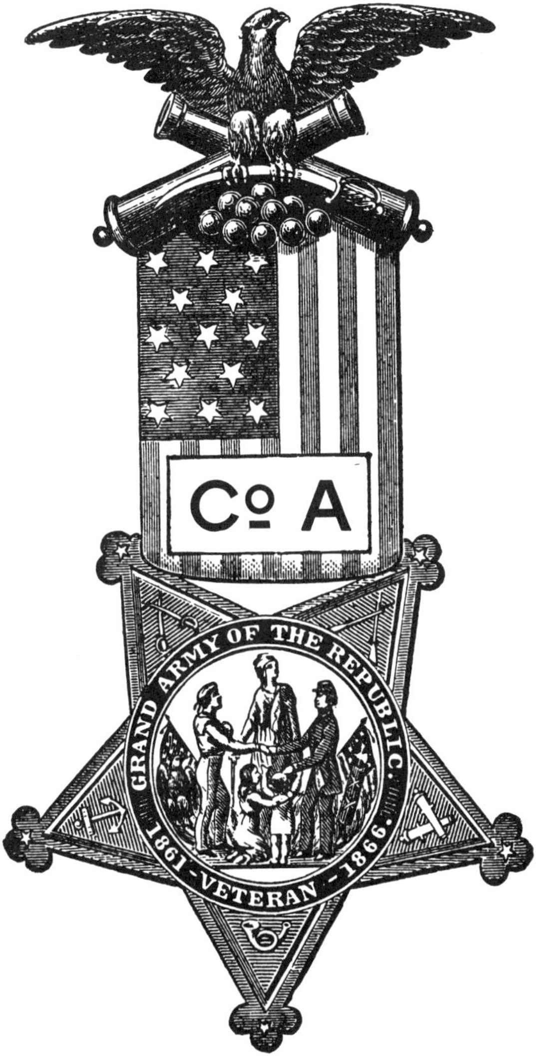
Co A
GRAND ARMY OF THE REPUBLIC
1861 · VETERAN · 1866

1864.

1893.

WM. H. FISHER,
Captain Co. "A."
1046 Warren Ave. W., Detroit, Mich.

Born at Mansfield, Ohio, August 22d, 1838; enlisted at Detroit, Mich., September 11th, 1862, as private in 7th Michigan Cavalry; was promoted to Sergeant of Co. "E," January 24th, 1863, First Lieutenant August 1st, 1863, and to Captain of Co. "A" October 12th, 1864; mustered out at Jackson, Mich., December 15th, 1865, and honorably discharged.

FIRST AND ONLY TWO DAYS' PICKET DUTY DURING MY TERM OF SERVICE.
By Captain W. H. Fisher.

This may seem strange, but nevertheless true. The positions and duties of the different offices I filled during my term of service were exempt from picket duty, and had it not so happened I think my term of service would have been cut short.

If there was any one duty that I was actually afraid of or detested that was "Picket Duty," especially at night. While you may not believe it, I was no nighthawk, not when it came to rambling around out in the fields and woods in the enemy's country, and alone at that.

I returned to the Regiment on the 20th of February, 1864, having been on leave of absence for forty days in Michigan. On reporting to the Colonel for duty I expected to resume at once my position as Acting Adjutant of the Regiment, a position I was holding before I left for the visit to my home, but on account of there being no Officer present in command of my Company ("E"), I was ordered to take command of it. I think it was the first morning after assuming charge of the Company that the Regiment was detailed for picket duty down on the Rapidan River. Companies "E" and "F," forming one battalion under command of Captain Carpenter, took charge of one part of the line, in fact, I do not remember after thirty-seven years where the balance of the Regiment was, but I presume it was on our right and left. We reached the outposts about 10 o'clock a. m. and at once relieved our friends who had been on duty for two days. Captain Carpenter, knowing I had been off duty for some time and not having been informed of my likes and dislikes of picket duties, ordered me to take charge of the picket line, or out-posts, in our front, which I, of course, was pleased to do, it being daytime, thinking that the night duty would fall on Lieutenant Dodge. Nothing of importance transpired during the day, so when night came on I came in to the reserve post, thinking I had the buldge on Lieutenant Dodge, anticipating a good night's sleep ahead of me, while poor Dodge would be dodging in and around the stumps and trees performing the duties as Officer on the out-posts. Soon after supper I curled myself up in my blanket, but had not laid there long when "Bang!" "Bang!" reached our ears from the out-post, and Captain Carpenter, being on the alert, soon had us all out and in line, and ordered me to proceed at once to discover the cause of the firing. I naturally objected, supposing that Lieutenant Dodge was taking his turn, but to my surprise and disgust he was sick and unable to ride, and knowing well the consequence of failing to obey orders I at once proceeded to the front, and was not long in finding the soldier that had given us the scare, as I for one was more than alarmed, and it being my first appearance on the picket line, all sorts of imaginations passed through my mind.

I think that was one of the longest nights of my army life. I do not believe I slept two hours all night, I remained at the outpost until morning and you may rest assured I cautioned each and every relief not to do any firing unless they were certain they saw or heard the enemy approaching his post.

The next day and night passed without any molestation from the enemy, and when the time came we were duly relieved of our two days' "Picket Duty," my first and last, for when we returned to camp I was again detailed as Acting Adjutant of the Regiment.

To me "Picket Duty" is the most lonesome, undesirable position any soldier can be assigned to, and still it is one of the most important places a soldier has to fill.

1864.

LUCIUS CARVER,
Lieutenant Co. "A."
Dead.

Born at Marshfield, Plymouth County, Mass., March 9th, 1840; enlisted at Boston, Suffolk County, Mass., November 23rd, 1862, as Private in Co. "M," 7th Michigan Cavalry; promoted to Sergeant Major June, 1863, and to Second Lieutenant March 22nd, 1864; killed in action at Front Royal, Va., August 16th, 1864, ending the life and career of a brave, heroic soldier and a courteous and manly young man. His remains were buried on the field of battle near where he fell and after the war were removed to his old home, where they now rest.

1864.   1901.

Edwin R. Havens,
Lieutenant Co. "A."

Lansing, Mich.

Born at Stafford, Genesee County, N. Y., May 25, 1842; enlisted at Buchanan, Berrien County, Mich., September 12th, 1862, as private (mustered as Sergeant) in Co. "A," 7th Michigan Cavalry; promoted to First Sergeant October 25th, 1863, and to Second Lieutenant May 25th, 1865; mustered out at Fort Leavenworth, Kan., December 15th, 1865; final muster out and discharge at Detroit, Mich., December 28th, 1865, and honorably discharged.

HOW MOSBY DESTROYED OUR TRAIN.
By Lieutenant E. R. Havens.

Our President has been very persistent in reminding me of a rash promise that I made to him, to contribute something to the collection of personal experiences during the years of our service, and has insisted upon the fulfillment of that promise.

Lieutenant Isham, on page 19 of his History of the Regiment, begins a paragraph with the following sentence:

"On the 29th of May, 1863, Mosby captured a train of cars near Carletts' Station by removing a rail."

As I saw the capture referred to in the above sentence, and being connected with certain events immediately following this, and as I remember it, the first skirmish in which a considerable portion of our Regiment was engaged, I have chosen the same for this article.

On the night of the 28th of May I was Sergeant of the Camp Guard, or picket around our camp, which, together with the First Vermont Cavalry, and a portion if not all of the 18th Pennsylvania Cavalary, we occupied at the bridge over Kettle Run, on the Orange & Alexandria Railroad, about two miles north of Warrenton Junction. My relief went on duty at twilight. When I had posted my last picket in the road at the west of the railroad and north of the camp, and was on my way to the reserve I heard a shot from the picket last posted. The names of the men on picket were: James Barber, Zeph. Wisner, and Henry or "Hank" Allen, all of Co. "A." I hastened to Barber's post to ascertain the cause of the firing, and was informed that two men on horseback had approached him, and on being hailed had ridden away to the left without halting, and thinking their actions suspicious he fired at them as they rode away. His story was but just told when from Wisner's post another shot was fired. His story was identical with Barber's, and was scarcely told when Allen's Burnside rang out on the night air. Hastening to his post, the same story was repeated, with the addition that as he fired his horse wheeled and started to run, but that he had soon brought it under control, and that as he returned to his post he saw one horse galloping away without a rider, while the rider on the other horse seemed to be holding his comrade across his saddle and both getting away. By this time it had become too dark to discern the tracks of horses or to satisfy myself that the dismounted rider has been wounded, as might have been indicated by discovering blood on the ground.

During the remainder of my tour of duty that night I did not lack for excitement or work, as it kept me in the saddle almost the entire time riding from one post to another to ascertain the causes for the many shots that were fired. About 1 o'clock next morning I was relieved by the other Sergeant at the reserve, and he was ordered to take eight men and patrol the railroad in the direction of Warrenton Junction, as far as the woods, a distance of about one mile. These woods, you will remember, extended north from near the Junction, half a mile or more, and acted as a screen for Mosby's attacks more than once during our acquaintance with that section of the "Old Dominion." I relieved the other Sergeant the next morning and posted the same relief that I had the night before just as a train loaded with supplies reached our station from Washington. On my way back to the reserve I halted at Allen's post, and was inspecting the ground trying to discover traces of his visitors of the evening before, when the train started on for the stations south of us. I was watching it as it neared the woods above referred to, and saw the locomotive as it swerved from a direct course on striking a misplaced rail, and also saw the smoke and heard the report from the little cannon by which the engine was disabled, and the skirmish before the firing of the train, and the retreat of the guerrillas. Immediately the camp was in preparation for the pursuit, permission to join the same being refused me because of the duty on which I was then engaged, so that I cannot describe the pursuit, or the battle that followed upon their overtaking the guerrillas that resulted in the dispersion of the band for the time being, with the capture of the cannon and several prisoners.

Among the prisoners taken, and who was at the time acting as cannonier, was a Louisianian named Montjoy, who was credited with a reputation as spy, scout, desperado, and an all-around bad man.

Scouting parties sent out that day captured other prisoners, so that we had under guard that night about thirty. The day following I was ordered to take a detail of several men from my Company and directed to report to Regimental headquarters for orders. On reporting I was directed to relieve the guard over the prisoners, and on arrival of the train for Washington, to remove the prisoners from the guard house to the train and escort them to Fairfax Court House, and turn them over to the Provost Marshal, and I was especially commanded to pay the strictest attention to the aforesaid Montjoy and to certainly deliver him at the Provost Marshal's headquarters, dead or alive. I did not fear an escape of any of the prisoners by daylight, but as the afternoon wore away I feared that night would overtake us before we could reach the Court House, as the three miles or more between the Station and the Court House must be made on foot, and I remembered one especially bad spot in the road where it passed through quite a deep cut, the sides and top of which were shaded by a heavy growth of timber, and you will all remember the darkness in that country at that season of the year was something impressive as well as oppressive, and it was at that point that I feared an attempt to escape would be made if made at all.

Now I was young in military experience and felt the importance of the responsible position I was then occupying. As it became dark I almost wished I was home, when I, picturing the desperate struggle that Montjoy would likely make to regain his freedom, and I could almost see myself a corpse by the roadside. But there was no way out of it and I was bound to make a bold face and bluff it out. As we neared the fateful spot I passed the word to my men in whispers, assigning to each his post in front or at the sides of the column, retaining as my bodyguards two in whom I had confidence as to their courage and devotion to duty, if not to myself, and placing the dreaded Montjoy in the rear of the column I took up my station by his side with my two guards. As we marched along the question came into my mind, what shall I do with my revolver, the only weapon that I carried. I first thought that I would carry it in my hand, cocked, and ready for action at the first move made by my prisoner to escape; then I argued that if I did and he happened to want a revolver, he could get mine easier than he could stop to buy one, as I would be no match for him in a physical contest, and that if I tried to shoot him I would be just as apt to shoot someone else, but if I carried it securely fastened in its holster he could not get it so easily, and I would not be so apt to kill some of my own men; so buttoning up my holster we marched along through the darkness, my nerves strained to the highest pitch and ready to break at every sound that was not clearly made by our marching feet. Never did anything look brighter to me than the lighter shadows of the night as we came out into more open country at the top of the hill without the loss of a prisoner or a life. The remainder of the march was without incident. I had found Captain Montjoy a very unassuming and sociable companion, and would enjoy meeting him to talk over the events of that day and night and laugh with him over the terrible fright he gave me.

On returning to camp next day, after dismissing my command, I repaired to headquarters to make my report and deliver the receipt of the Provost Marshal for the prisoners placed in my care, and expecting to receive a "Well done, good and faithful servant," but Oh, what a fall was there! I was met by the Lieutenant-Colonel who, upon learning that I had taken away the prisoners the day before, demanded to know why I did not kill him; why I did not let somebody else kill him, etc.

I finally found out that some unregenerate "Mushrat" without the fear of that lake which is said to be the "Portion of all liars" before him, had circulated the story that while transferring the prisoners from the guard house to the train the dreaded Montjoy had attacked me, and tried to get my pistol; that he had me down on the ground and nearly dead before he could be overpowered, and that when one of my men had attempted to shoot him I had forbidden it, all of which had caused the good Colonel to feel very wroth towards the said Montjoy, and correspondingly so towards your humble servant.

1864   1895

HENRY L. ANTHONY,
Sergeant Co. "A."
Sturgis, Mich.

Born November 9th, 1843, at Bedford, Calhoun County, Mich.; enlisted at Bedford, Calhoun County, State of Michigan, September 8th, 1862, as private in Co. "A," in the 7th Michigan Cavalry; was promoted to Commissary Sergeant October 24th, 1864, and First Sergeant, June 17th, 1865, all of Co. "A"; was wounded at Buckland Mills, Va., October 19th, 1863, and mustered out on December 15th, 1865, at Jackson, Mich., and honorably discharged.

Comrade Anthony has succeeded as a man of business and high social prominence, having advanced to and holds the responsible position of Cashier of the National Bank of Sturgis, Mich.; has been honored by the Masonic Fraternity of Michigan, having passed through all the grades of office in the Grand Commandery, serving as Grand Commander during 1894 and 1895, and is now serving his third year as Grand Recorded. Such honors come to but few.

REMINISCENCE.
By H. L. Anthony.

Upon the urgent request of our President of the 7th Michigan Cavalry Association, I in an unguarded moment promised to write something for the "Facial History" of the members of the old 7th. After the swift flight of nearly forty years, when we were factors in suppressing an armed rebellion, it is extremely difficult for one not accustomed to such work to give names, dates, places and events which served to make a personal or Regimental history in those days, and doubly so when one's thoughts have been earnestly directed in other channels. As I look back through the dimness of memory's vision I do not recall any startling or especially blood-curdling incidents in my personal career as a soldier for "Uncle Sam."

Regardless of what I may have thought in my earlier days, I have learned to know that the war might possibly have been conducted to a successful final had I not entered the army at all, still I know that the material and the mettle that composed the 7th Cavalry was the equal of any Regiment from Michigan. In fact, they were the equal in every way of any Regiment in that great army that finally broke the back of the Rebellion. And now as the shadows begin to lengthen toward the sunset of life and I look back upon the service rendered during those long and sacrificial years, I remember much that is worthy of our pride and glory and little for regret and insofar as any part that I bore in that service I have the satisfaction of knowing that I always obeyed the call of my commanding officers to any duty imposed upon me and was to the best of my ability faithfully performed.

The men who composed my Regiment *ought* to be remembered by a grateful country as among those who made the names of Kilpatrick, Custer and Sheridan immortal and whose record for bravery and heroic service to their country will never die.

1863.   1901.

R. MARSHALL BELLINGER,

Sergeant Co. "A."

54 Rose St., Battle Creek, Mich.

Born in Barry County, Mich., August 4th, 1845; enlisted at Battle Creek, Mich., September 15th, 1862, as Private in Co. "A," 7th Michigan Cavalry; promoted to Sergeant June 28th, 1864; mustered out at Fort Leavenworth, Kansas, December 15th, 1865, and honorably discharged, after participating in 36 engagements.

INCIDENTS OF THE CAMPAIGN OF 1864.

By R. Marshall Bellinger.

At the Battle of Yellow Tavern, May 11th, 1864, our Regiment was ordered to charge up a hill by column of fours through a cut, but meeting with such fierce resistance the cut soon became so blocked with dead men and horses that further advance was impossible, and we were then ordered to dismount and fight on foot. As we charged up the hill and through the timber we came to a cleared field. Comrades Adams, Burk and myself of Co. "A" were together; "there might have been others with us, but do not remember." To our right and front we could see what I took to be the 1st Michigan Cavalry charging mounted Rebels; to our left on a hill about twenty-five rods from us was a group of Confederate officers mounted and standing still, displaying a fine battle flag. Adams said, "Let's go for that flag," and suiting the action to the suggestion, started to climb the fence; I pulled him back, saying, "We can reach them from here," and taking aim across the fence I fired. An officer fell forward on his horse, others of the group took hold of him and immediately rode to the rear over the hill out of sight, Adams remarking, "You have winged one of them." There has been much speculation as to who shot the Rebel General Jeb. Stuart, who was wounded that day, dying the next. The 1st Vermont, 5th and 7th Michigan all have claimants. If General Stuart was shot with a revolver bullet or by a mounted soldier, I have no claim, but if he was shot with a carbine bullet while mounted and standing with the group with the battle flag, I have every reason to believe that my bullet did the work, as it certainly hit some officer, be it honor, murder, or whatever it may be called.

At the Battle of Smithfield, August, 1864, Co. "A" was thrown across the river, "I think the Opequon," through a covered bridge; advancing about eighty rods we were deployed on a ridge parallel with the river. I was on the extreme left of the line and the country to my left and front was open, on my right and front, timber. I soon heard a bullet zip by, but could not see where it came from. I soon saw a puff of smoke from a tree top about forty rods in front of me, and a bullet struck the ground about four feet to my left. Dismounting and laying my carbine across my saddle, I fired. The next bullet from my friend struck the ground at my feet, the next hit my horse, inflicting only a slight wound. We exchanged six or seven shots when I saw my Confederate friend slide down the tree and hostilities ceased. As I was a very good shot and my Confederate friend certainly was, I rather enjoyed the scrap and paid little attention to the rest of the line. Hearing rapid firing on my right, I mounted and looking to the right and rear I saw our men just entering the bridge and a number of Confederates right on their heels. I made straight for the river, about thirty rods below the bridge, when five or six Rebels started to head me off, firing their revolvers and yelling, "Surrender, you Yank!" On nearing the river I saw that the bank was about four feet above the water, so throwing my feet out of the stirrups and giving my horse both spurs, he made a great leap into the river, landing in deep water and pulling for the other bank, which was low. As I rode out the Rebels on the opposite bank were still firing their revolvers at me, so I gave them one parting shot, not stopping to see where my bullet went, but rode up the hill and joined the Regiment, dripping wet.

Adjutant Charlie Pratt, formerly of Co. "A," said: "I want to congratulate you on your escape; I watched your race for the river and remarked to the Colonel that you were a goner this time and it looked that way to me for a time."

In October, 1864, Sheridan's Army lay stretched across the Shenandoah Valley on the north bank of Cedar Creek facing south. On the night of the 18th our Regiment was detailed for picket on the right flank. After posting our pickets well in front on the south side of the Creek, we went into camp on a hillside on the north bank. After eating our supper and feeding our horses, everything being quiet, we went to sleep, leaving our horses saddled and bridled. During the night the Rebel Infantry quietly stole through our picket line in front of our

Infantry, marched along the bank of Cedar Creek between the picket line and our army and created no disturbance until they struck the camp of the 7th Michigan Cavalry.

The first thing I heard was a volley of musketry at close range and the zipping of bullets. Every one was on their feet and mounting their horse in a moment; officers were shouting for their companies to fall in; evidently the order was understood for us to fall back, as everybody broke for the rear. It was just at daybreak, but so foggy we could see little but could hear a good deal. We were in a pocket formed by a high bluff on the west, a board fence on the north, and the Rebels on the south and east. There was a narrow gap in the fence near the bluff and all seemed anxious to be the first one through it. I was riding a horse at that time known as "Dan Rice," on account of his circus performing habits, which consisted of his balking or standing still and kicking when first mounted. Whether he thought he would show more courage than the men and stand his ground and kick the Rebels back into the Creek or what, I never knew, but he stood still and kicked, and the more I spurred him the higher he kicked. The Rebels were getting very close for I could hear their voices very plainly as one said, "There is a good horse, Sam, catch him." I do not know whether he meant my horse or not, but do not think Sam would have dared gotten near enough to Dan to catch him while he was kicking. All this time the Rebels were advancing and firing; bullets went zipping past me, and it seemed to me that every one of them hit the fence near me. "I can almost hear them now, over thirty-seven years later." The thoughts of Andersonville made the situation desperate, and having my carbine in my hand I struck Dan on the head which knocked him down. I stuck to the saddle and when he regained his feet he was ready to go, and so was I. Riding through the gap, I circled to the right and soon found the Regiment in line on higher and more open ground, actively taking part in the great battle which has gone down in history as the Battle of Cedar Creek.

1896.

RAY T. STREETER,
Corporal Co. "A."
Marcellus, Cass Co., Mich.

Born May 28th, 1846, at Emmett, Calhoun County, Mich.; enlisted at Battle Creek, Calhoun County, Mich., November 15th, 1862, as private in Co. "A," 7th Michigan Cavalry; was promoted to Corporal, 1865; was mustered out at Fort Leavenworth, Kan., December, 1865, and honorably discharged.

INSIDE THE REBEL LINES AND NOT CAPTURED.
By Ray T. Streeter.

At Buckland Mills, October 19th, 1863, our Regiment was sent into the woods as skirmishers, the woods being dense, we could only see a little ways in any direction. I was the last man on the left of Co. "A," and do not think that there were any other troops at my left. The Rebels were quite thick in our front and the bullets came through the brush lively. We had been on this line for some time when on looking around I could not see any of our boys—they had been recalled and I did not know it.

I immediately started in the direction that I supposed they had gone, but got tangled in the thick brush, and had to get off my horse and lead him. I finally got out in the open, but could not see any of our men, so started for the pike and struck it a short distance from the bridge. When I got on the pike I could see the bridge, and on the bridge and beyond it I could see lots of Rebels. I crossed the pike and started up the stream, thinking that I could find a place to cross. For some distance up the stream the ground was quite low. A hundred rods or so from the pike the high land came down to the stream, making a sort of promontory. Farther up the stream I could see a crossing place, in which was a wagon and an ambulance or two with the Rebels all around them. At this instant I heard someone yell "Surrender!" and looking around saw a dozen Rebel Cavalry coming down the ridge; turned my horse down around the point to the stream—the bank was fully six feet high—but my horse took the jump and landed in the water pretty nearly all over. Fortune favored me, for the bank on the opposite side was low, and the horse had no trouble getting out. While we were still in the stream the Rebels rode onto the point of the ridge and commenced to shoot at me and yell at me to halt. It was only a couple of rods from the edge of the stream to the thick brush, and as soon as I got into it I was all right. It was only a narrow strip of woods; then I came out into a big field. In front of me and nearly in the middle of the field a Regiment of Rebel Cavalry was crossing. I turned to the left, followed the edge of the field to another piece of woods and went into them. Passing through them and still keeping to the left I came out onto a large plantation. Off to the right was a house, and near it was our troops, as I could see by their uniforms. I started for them, but had gone only a rod or so when I saw the Rebel Regiment that I had seen in the field come out into the open ground, form in squadrons and charged our men that were near the house, and they had a regular mix-up. I did not stop to look on but sheared further to the left, making good time going about half a mile, when I came to a line of our Infantry with battery in position.

You may be assured I was glad to see them. I tell you they looked good. I soon joined our Regiment, and felt very grateful that I was on my way to Richmond.

1900.

OSCAR I. HUNT,

Corporal Co. "A."

Sumner, Gratiot County, Mich.

Born November 15, 1844, at Brookland, Lenawee Co., Mich.; enlisted at Battle Creek, Calhoun Co., Mich., September 10, 1862, as Private in Co. "A,' 7th Michigan Cavalry; was promoted to Corporal May 1, 1865; was mustered out at Jackson, Mich., December 15, 1865, and honorably discharged.

OUR FIRST MARCH FROM WASHINGTON TO FAIRFAX.

By Oscar I. Hunt.

I shall never forget our first crossing the long bridge and then the slimy slump of the horses' feet in the mud as we enjoyed the midnight scenery. We arrived at Fairfax about sunrise, and pitched our dog tents in the mud and the beautiful blanket of snow. That night Major Huston came around with his key. Of course it was not a door key—the boys called it whiskey.

All at once we heard the order, Hark, Mosby, Mosby hurry up, for God's sake men, hurry up. We all rushed to horse and after taking a little ride got to camp, but Mosby was like Pat's flee, he was not there; at any rate we did not get our fingers on him or our eyes either, so we bid farewell to the old cuss and went back to quarters—it was only a false alarm.

In snow, water and mud we made a bed; our blankets were soft, if they were wet and cold.

1865.   1901.

JOHN LINDSEY MACDONALD,

Co. "A."

Scriven, Minn.

Born at Rochester, Monroe County, N. Y., March 20th, 1849; enlisted at Flint, Genesee County, Mich., Feb. 18th, 1865, as Private in Co. "A," 7th Michigan Cavalry; mustered out at Fort Leavenworth, Kansas, December 15th, 1865, and honorably discharged.

REMINISCENCE.

By J. L. MacDonald.

In March, 1865, I was one of a squad sent into Loudon Valley, Va., to capture some Rebel officers that were reported to be at Leesburg. We reached there at night and made a capture of a few prisoners.

The next morning we started on our return to Harper's Ferry. Comrade Hammond of Co. "A" and myself decided to make a tour of inspection on our own account; we had not gone more than two miles when we saw a Rebel officer coming toward us finely mounted. We wanted him and horse; he anticipating our intention rode up to a large farm house. dismounted and entered in great haste. We dismounted, keeping our horses between us and the house and succeeded in reaching his horse and leading him off. We had not gone far when several shots were fired after us, but we kept on our course until we came to a cross-road, where we met a colored woman who informed us that Mosby's men, under command of Captain White, were in pursuit of our detachment. We put spurs to our horses and were soon at the bridge near Waterford. There we met a young Quaker lady whom we knew and who informed us that Mosby's men were in possession of the town and entreated us not to go through, but there was no other way for us to go. We could see through a thin fringe of trees that lay between us and the town of one street, several men moving about. We decided to take a desperate chance and dash through by forcing our horses to their greatest speed and firing our carbines as we went. Everybody got off the street for us, but as soon as they recovered from their surprise several volleys were fired after us. On looking back we saw mounted men after us and a desperate race was kept up for a few miles, when they gave up the chase and we soon reached Harper's Ferry. The Provost General on learning of the fine horse we had captured ordered his guards to take him from us, notwithstanding my protest and the risk we had incurred to possess him.

On July 5th, 1865, our Regiment broke camp on the Big Blue River in Kansas. We began our march about three o'clock in the morning, as we had to reach Fort Kearney on the Platte River, which was nearly forty miles ahead of us, before we could go into camp again, as there was no water for ourselves or horses until we reached the Platte.

The day was extremely hot and our canteens were soon empty; we rode all day in that terrible heat and our sufferings and thirst became unbearable. About three p. m. we came to a ranch where there was a well and my Company broke ranks for it. I was one of the first to reach it, and in lowering the bucket it got caught on some timbers. I got on the rope to go down and unfasten it while comrades held the windlass. I had gone down but a few feet when the rope broke, letting me fall to the bottom, a distance of over one hundred feet. There was only about two feet of water. I was unconscious for a time, but the cold water no doubt brought me too, when I discovered that my comrades had lowered a rope which I tied around me and was hauled up and assisted to mount my horse; I rode with great difficulty to camp, and suffered for many days after.

In about a week after the accident we reached Julesburg, Colo. Ter., where on a very dark night I was put on picket. Was relieved at midnight and went to my quarters and was soon fast asleep, but was soon disturbed by firing from the picket and the hurried command to fall in. In my crippled condition I was prevented from moving fast and could not find my carbine, my Company was in line and I becoming desperate drew my sabre and took my place. The darkness prevented the officers knowing my sad predicament, so I escaped censure.

In August, 1865, I was one of a detail of eight men sent

to guard a supply train from Fort Halleck to Bridgers Pass, Wyoming.

On our return trip we had just gotten through Rattle Snake Pass when we noticed a cloud of dust rising to our right, which we concluded was caused by a herd of buffalos moving in that direction. We had gone but a few miles when we discovered our mistake, as we now realized that a large band of warriors were aiming to intercept us before we could reach Fort Halleck. We urged our horses to their utmost speed, but the Indians were fast gaining on us. My horse began to give out and I was falling to the rear and the Indians coming nearer every moment. It began to look hopeless for me, but I pushed on and reached the top of a ridge in view of the Fort, about a mile away, which gave me courage and my horse seemed to be inspired by my feelings and plunged forward as if he had received new life; in a few minutes I was quite near the Fort and safe.

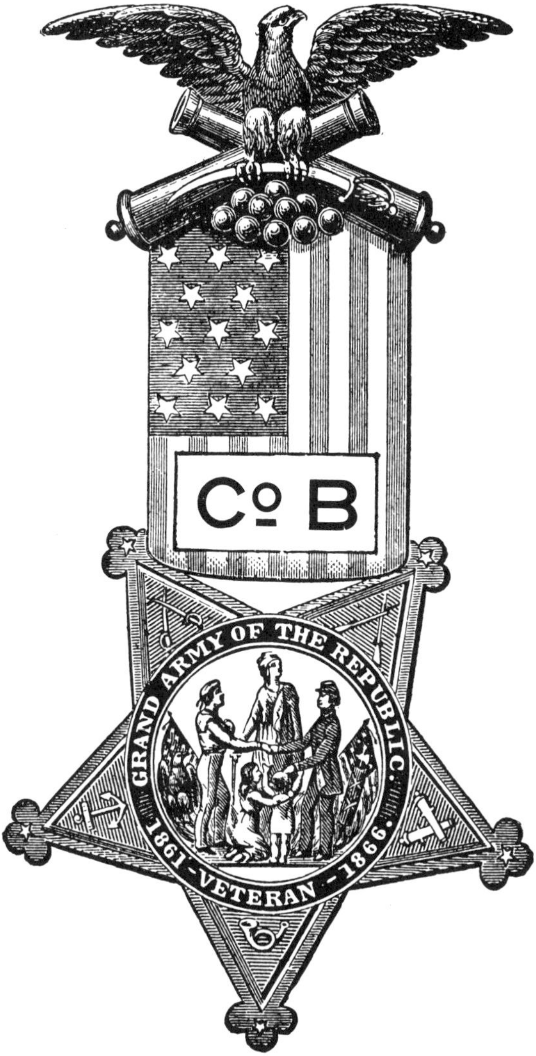
Co B
GRAND ARMY OF THE REPUBLIC.
1861 - VETERAN - 1866.

1863.

Elliott Gray,

Lieutenant Co. "B."

Dead.

Born at Tecumseh, Lenawee County, Mich., May 22nd, 1833; enlisted at Tecumseh, Lenawee County, Mich., September 4th, 1862, as Private in Co. "B," 7th Michigan Cavalry; promoted to First Lieutenant October 15th, 1862, and served on General Custer's Staff eighteen months; wounded in action at Williamsport, Md., July 8th, 1863; resigned February 28th, 1865, at Washington, D. C., and honorably discharged; died March 22nd, 1899, at Tecumseh, Mich.

1900.

Henry F. Thomas,
Lieutenant Co. "B."

Allegan, Mich.

Born at Tompkins, Jackson County, Mich., December 17th, 1843; enlisted at Eaton Rapids, Eaton County, Mich., August 7th, 1862, as private in Co. "D," 7th Michigan Cavalry; promoted to Sergeant, Co. "D," December 15th, 1862; First Sergeant, Co. "D," May 1st, 1863; Second Lieutenant, Co. "B," July 31st, 1864; mustered out at Fort Leavenworth, Kansas, December 15th, 1865, and honorably discharged.

1863.   1900.

Dr. Adelbert H. Weston,
Sergeant Co. "B,"
330 Colorado Ave., Colorado City, Col.

Born in Watertown Township, Clinton County, Mich., January 30th, 1842; enlisted at Maple Rapids, Clinton County, Mich., October 20th, 1862, as Private in Co. "B," 7th Michigan Cavalry; promoted to Corporal and a short time after to Sergeant, was promoted to Hospital Steward in June, 1865; mustered out at Fort Leavenworth, Kansas, December 12th, 1865, and honorably discharged.

A SHOCK.
By A. H. Weston.

At the Battle of the Wilderness, May 6th and 7th, 1864, as all our boys in that battle will remember, in the first charge our Regiment made there, we went in in rear of the Regiment in front. When we returned and were reforming, a piece of shell struck the ground in front of where I was, bounded, and hit my left arm between elbow and shoulder, numbing it; I remarked to some of the boys, "I guess I am cropped." At about the same time my right hand comrade was shot through the hand and Sergeant Gregg ordered us both back under cover. We dismounted and retired, and as each of us had one hand to use, we wet his handkerchief and tied up his hand, then turned attention to my arm, which we found only had a big bruise on it. I can assure you it was an agreeable surprise to find that my left arm was still left intact and all right. I was soon in saddle and back in my place.

1863.   1902.

Wm. Edward House,

Corporal Co. "B."

108 Portage St., Kalamazoo, Mich.

Born at Gaines, Orleans County, N. Y., December 21st, 1844; enlisted at Tecumseh, Lenawee County, Mich., September 29th, 1862, as Private in Co. "B," 7th Michigan Cavalry; promoted to Corporal May 1st, 1865; mustered out at Fort Leavenworth, Kansas, December 15th, 1865, and honorably discharged.

IN SHENANDOAH VALLEY, 1864.
By Wm. Edward House.

In 1864 while our Regiment was marching near Berryville in the Shenandoah Valley, the Rebs opened a battery on us, the first shell went over our heads and burst about sixty feet beyond us, then the Colonel gave the command "Halt!" I knew I was in range of their guns and hardly had time to think when another shell burst right in our ranks, killing our bugler, wounding several and causing my horse and four others to go down in a heap. I was not hit, but my horse got a piece of shell through the neck and fell so quickly that my foot was caught under him; I could not get out and called for help, and the Orderly Sergeant of my Company came and helped me, which saved me from being captured. I left blankets, overcoat, haversack and horse for the Rebs, only saving my Spencer and ammunition, nevertheless the Johnnies gave me a parting shot as I went over the hill and out of their sight. Being dismounted I was in a bad condition, as I could not keep up with the Regiment, so remained back with an Infantry Regiment that night. The next morning I came across another Cavalry man who had lost his horse and we decided to go to the Dismounted Camp, which was twenty miles away through a country where we were liable to meet and be captured by Mosby's men. We saw where they had camped that night and met an old man, who said he thought we were taking desperate chances. We marched right through Charlestown as brave as lions, men on the hotel steps got out of sight as soon as they saw us coming, but I have often thought they would have captured or killed us had they known we were alone. Before leaving the town we called at a house and ordered something to eat. The old darkey cook was badly frightened; she gave us half a chicken pie which was good and it did not take us long to get outside of it. She said, "May the good Lord save and protect you, massa." We continued our march, passing through a small settlement, and when darkness came on went into an old blacksmith shop and remained there all night; starting early the next morning we soon came to our outpickets. They thought we were deserters and sent us under escort to Headquarters, where we were soon identified and given quarters. We remained there two weeks, then drew horses and returned to our Regiment. The command was just ready for the Sheppardstown Raid and in less than two hours I was where the bullets were flying like hail. We got into very hot quarters and were glad to get out, as they gave us a very warm reception.

To me the most vivid recollection of the War of the Rebellion was the Battle of Cedar Creek, October 19th, 1864.

I believe the entire Regiment was on duty that eventful night. I was on picket the forepart of the night, being relieved at midnight and went to reserve camp, made some coffee and then rolled up in my blankets and went to sleep. I do not know how long I had been sleeping when I dreamed that I heard the pickets firing. It was so real that it wakened me and I got up and bridled my horse; in a minute I heard three shots, then I was sure there was danger, so wakened those who were still sleeping. While most of them got up, others did not, and said, "Oh, it is only a false alarm." Billy Kemp and I stood with our hands on our saddles ready to mount when all at once we heard the order, "Forward, charge!" and saw a streak of fire which almost encircled us. I saw at once that the creek was our only escape, so Billy and I took the lead, his horse pushing down the lane fence that led to the creek. There were bluffs along the creek about fifteen or twenty feet high and a path ran down the bank, so we had to go single file. We had not gone far when we saw a line of men on the bluff ready to receive us, so we put spurs to our horses, and when we got opposite of them they fired a volley, but as it was quite dark their aim being poor, only one man was hit and he in the arm. We moved about one hundred rods and then up the hill, halted, counted up, and found we had one officer and ten men, the officer being Captain Sergeant; my impression is that it was about three o'clock in the morning. We soon heard the Rebels coming and could hear the officers giving orders in their effort to capture the Infantry Reserve, but the Reserve being ready for them waited until the advance got within about ten rods when they gave the Rebs a volley which staggered them and they broke and ran. They rallied and came back the second time, got the same dose, and retired. We waited until daybreak, when we heard the attack on the main line, then we started for the fray. We had no idea what had become of the rest of our Regiment, so we reported to a command of Cavalry and were assigned as reserve to a battery, and a hot place it was. We could see the Army retreating, running like a flock of sheep, except the 6th Corps, who held and stood together and fought like tigers. Then came the conquering hero, General Sheridan, and what a change. The men began yelling and throwing up their hats and the Rebels thought we had received reinforcements, so stopped firing and began to prepare for defense; then the tide turned and everyone knows the result. I know I slept in my old camp that night, but if I remember rightly there were only eight of the eleven camped together that night.

At daybreak on the morning that Lee surrendered, "April 9th, 1865," having been on the skirmish line all night, I thought I would have time to make some coffee, but just as a fire was started the pickets came running in and said, "Lee's Army is advancing." We were ordered to mount and double quick around a piece of woods, drew up in line and dismounted and fought on foot, every fourth man holding the horses. When I dismounted I missed my cartridge box. I went to the Captain and reported to him that I had left my cartridge box on the other side of the woods; he said, "It isn't over forty rods through the woods, better try and get it." I was anxious to have the cartridge box, for it was one I had captured from a Rebel. I got it all right and had just buckled it on when I heard some one yell, "Surrender, you Yank!" Looking around and seeing a number of Rebs with their guns at their shoulders covering me, I thought of the losing of the $60.00 in my pocket and my clothes, and at the same time noticed a large tree just in front. I felt impelled to jump behind it. Guess it was the quickest move I ever made in my life and as I reached it they fired a volley but never touched me; then I ran like a deer through the woods, they firing at me until I got nearly through. When I got back to where I left my Company they were out of sight, but found a pony there, mounted him, but he began bucking, so I dismounted and started on the trail of my Company; had not gone far when someone to my left said, "Where you going?" I motioned to him to keep quiet, and I sneaked along just as though I was after someone, and it worked all right. He was one of the Rebel line on the bluff not more than twenty rods away. I soon rounded the end of the bluff, out of their sight and in sight of our lines. I soon saw General Custer and Staff ride out to meet a flag of truce, then I felt safe and made good time and was soon with my Company, they supposing I had been captured. Very soon General Grant's Staff met General Lee and the Rebels all along the line were throwing up their hats and cheering, and soon we were all together shaking hands and rejoicing, for we all knew the war was over.

Co. C

1863.   1901.

BARTHOLOMEW GRIFFIN,

Quartermaster Sergeant Co. "C."

Carrollton, Saginaw Co., Mich.

Born at City of Ottawa, Ont., March 1st, 1843; enlisted at Saginaw, Saginaw County, Mich., August 11th, 1862, as Private in Co. "C," 7th Michigan Cavalry; was promoted to Corporal, 1862, and to Quarter-Master Sergeant of Co. "C," January 15th, 1865; was taken prisoner at Robinson River, Va., October 9th, 1863, and was taken to Libby Prison, Pemberton Castle and Belle Isle, Va., for five months, was in Andersonville, Ga., seven months, escaped from there January 1865, and was mustered out at Fort Leavenworth, Kan., October 20th, 1865, and was honorably discharged.

1900.

JAMES SMITH,
Commissary Sergeant Co. "C."
New Lothrop, Mich.

Born May 2nd, 1835, at Mansfield, Richland County, Ohio; enlisted at Flushing, Genesee County, Mich., October 3rd, 1862, as Private in Co. "C," 7th Michigan Cavalry; was promoted to Corporal in 1863 and to Commissary Sergeant July, 1865; was mustered out at Fort Leavenworth, Kan., December 15, 1865, and honorably discharged.

1895.

David B. Rose,
Sergeant Co. "C."

Reese, Tuscola Co., Mich.

Born August 10, 1827, in Ulster County, N. Y.; enlisted at Junietta, Tuscola County, Mich., September 10th, 1862, as Private in the Co. "C," 7th Michigan Cavalry; was promoted to Corporal in Co. "C" in the fall of 1862, and made First Sergeant in Co. "C" in November of 1863; was wounded at the Battle of Gettysburg on July 3rd, 1863, being shot in the shoulder and remained in the hospital until November; was captured at Trevilian's Station, Va., June 11th, 1864; was in prison about ten months, being taken to Libby, thence to Millen, Savannah, and Thomasville, Ga., thence to Andersonville, and from there was exchanged and honorably discharged at Detroit, Mich., August 12th, 1865.

MAJOR GRANGER'S DEATH.
By David B. Rose.

I was looking over the history of our Regiment this morning and came across the account of Major Granger's death. This suggested to me that I write my version of his death.

The Major was not shot full of holes, but as I remember, only two bullet holes marred his body, a saber cut over his eye and one in the left breast near the heart.

You ask how I know this. I was the man that found the Major dead on the field, lying, perhaps, one hundred rods from the cut in the road where my Company made a charge and was forced to retreat down the hill into a woods, where we dismounted. Just at this time Lieutenant Birney ordered me to take the dismounted men and horses to the rear. I told him that I was going with the boys to the front, and I did, after obeying Lieutenant Birney's next order, which was to send the men back under a competent man.

When I got on the hill, through the cut I saw our Regiment far to the left, and front, still after the Rebels. On my right lay a large field free from all obstruction. On this field I saw a black object lying. I wondered what it was so far from the track taken by the combatants, and decided to investigate. I hastened to the spot and found, as I feared, a dead soldier. Dismounted, and found that it was our loved Major, still and cold in death.

Yes, Major Granger lay dead before me. Soon two horsemen came galloping up to where I was. The first thing they said was, "Who is that, Sergeant?" "It is Major Granger," I replied. "Major Granger, my God! is that so?" "Yes, it is so." The Surgeon told me to give it to him and he would give it to other, an Officer of our Regiment, name not remembered. They then told me to examine the pockets. I did and found that they had been searched and nothing left but a short piece of comb. The two riders were Assistant Surgeon Dr. G. R. Richards, the

the Major's wife. Before leaving me, I asked them what I should do, they told me to get men enough to carry the Major to the rear near Yellow Tavern, and guard his remains until further orders. Again, I was left alone, but stragglers began to come within sight, giving me hope to soon get away with my charge, but before I did I had another visitor, who rode up all alone, asking the same question as did the others who had just left me. The Officer was none other than General Custer himself. My answer to him was Major Granger. He exclaimed, "My God, is Granger dead; can it be!" He wanted to see his face and where he had been wounded. I uncovered the dead face, pointed to a wound over the left eye, then bared his breast and showed him a wound near the heart, this one made by a bullet. The one over the eye was a saber wound. The General believed the Major had been murdered as did the other Officers, and seemed to feel badly over the sad affair. He was not afraid to talk, even though he was only talking to a Sergeant, and this is what he said:

"I sat just where I could see every move made by the Major at the time of the charge, and I never saw a man go more galiantly about the work before him than he did. He was a splendid man; too bad, too bad."

As he left me he gave me the same orders about taking care of the remains as did the other Officers, which I can assure you was most faithfully obeyed. When the General left me I supposed that this would be the last that I would see of him, but I was mistaken, for before I got enough men together to carry such a heavy man as the Major was, General Custer with his whole staff rode up to take a last look at the noble dead.

The General had been superintending planting a battery to play on the Rebs near by. As he rode up he said, "Sergeant, I am back again; please let these gentlemen see the Major." Again I uncovered his face and every one drew up to his side and took a long, last look. All spoke words of praise, and regretted the great loss we had sustained in his death.

While yet the Officers were viewing the dead a rifle shot or shell came most uncomfortably close to us, upon which one of the Staff Officers rode up to the General and said, "General, our flag is too conspicuous, the Rebs have got our range. What shall be done?" "Let the flag retire," which it did and the Staff was not driven away, but retired when it suited them.

On leaving the General said, "Sergeant, don't forget the orders I have given you," and I was left in charge of the dead again, but soon got men enough and left for the rear to obey the first and the last order I ever had the honor of receiving from the gallant Custer.

They were faithfully obeyed, I can assure you, and the Major was buried where history states.

1863.   1899.

WM. GLOVER GAGE,

Corporal Co. "C."

Saginaw, E. S., Mich.

Born April 11th, 1847, at Italy Hill, Yates County, N. Y.; enlisted at East Saginaw, Saginaw County, Mich., August 1st, 1862, as Private in Co. "C," 7th Michigan Cavalry; was mustered as Corporal, Acting Sergeant and Quartermaster-Sergeant of Company most of time; was taken prisoner at Gettysburg, Pa., July 3d, 1863, paroled about August 6th, 1863, at Richmond, Va., sent to Annapolis, Md., and returned to Regiment without exchange September, 1863 (was in Libby Prison the last few days, before that in prison at Stanton, Va.); was mustered out at East Saginaw, Mich., March 17th, 1865, and honorably discharged.

RECONNAISSANCE AROUND WARRENTON JUNCTION, VA.
By William Glover Gage.

When our Regiment was stationed at Warrenton Junction, in the spring of 1863, it was ordered out one day for a ride we knew not where. After proceeding some distance the Regiment was divided into two detachments which took different routes. Our detachment proceeded along a well travelled highway in a northwesterly direction for some distance, when a Sergeant and some ten or twelve men were detached from our Company and directed to follow a country cross-road, no one but the Sergeant knew whither.

Frequent skirmishes with the members of the redoubtable Mosby's Command had taught us to expect an enemy to fire at us from any bush or fence corner on the road, and we were careful to keep a good lookout for Rebs. As soon as the Sergeant started on the by-road a Corporal was sent some 200 yards ahead to act as advanced guard.

We had not proceeded far on this road before the Corporal recognized it as a road to the Marstellis or Marcellis farm-house of which we had visited on other occasions.

No unusual incident occurred until our advance reached the brow of a hill some 800 or 1,000 yards from the grove which surrounded the Marstellis Mansion, in true old Virginian style.

This hill was perhaps forty or fifty feet above the valley below, and the road by which we were approaching the house dropped into this valley and ran along a level stretch and then gradually rose to the elevation upon which the house was situated, and was in full view from the grove surrounding the buildings.

From our point of vantage we discovered that the grounds and grove surrounding the buildings were literally alive with horsemen and it was soon quite apparent that our presence was unexpected and that it was causing considerable commotion among the people in the grove.

Meantime the advance guard was gradually drawing nearer to the house and straining his eyes to determine whether the excited horsemen, within the grove, were friends or foes. At a distance they appeared to be clad in grey, and when the advance of the Sergeant's party was about 500 yards from the grove several of the men emerged from there and came tearing down the road at full speed, revolvers in hand.

The Corporal in advance glanced back to see if the Sergeant would render assistance, when much to his amazement, he saw the Sergeant with all of his men but two skirting the brink of the hill in full flight.

We took in the situation at a glance, for we had no time to do more, but we will never forget the picture of that Sergeant as we looked up from below, outlined against the sky, leading his men in a mad headlong rush for safety. He was putting spurs to his big bay charger, whose head was stretched out level with his body and his tail straight out behind, and his men a close second.

The Sergeant had already lost his cap and he and some of his men were freeing themselves as rapidly as possible of all impediments, such as canteens, haversack and the like. Whether any of them lightened themselves of their arms and ammunition we never knew, as we did not visit the grounds after the "action."

One of the Sergeant's party who was acting as rear guard, and one other of his men staid by the Corporal and they at once turned their attention to the horsemen who were dashing down upon them, hoping for some fortunate turn of affairs by which they might escape from death or prison, but fully resolved to fight it out to the end.

When the horsemen from the house came within hailing distance some of their forms appeared familiar, notwithstanding they were disguised by ponchoes thrown over their shoulders, for it had been raining. When the Corporal's party recognized that one at least was a member of their own Company, detailed on the Colonel's provost, they were greatly relieved.

The men from the house seemed equally pleased to find that the Corporal and comrades were not an advance guard of Rebs. It was then learned that the men at the house were all members of our Regiment and that they had reached there by a different road some time earlier.

The reason they appeared at a distance to be clad in grey was because many of them had thrown old grain sacks over their shoulders to protect them from the recent rain. At the house it was learned that when our troops had approached it several shots had been fired from the windows and a member of the Regiment had been mortally wounded and was then dying in one of the rooms.

The Rebels had escaped to the timber which lay near the house on one side. Soon after the Corporal and party reached the house a Corporal of Co. "E," whose name was Raymond, saw a man prowling along through the timber crouching near the ground in an effort to avoid observation. Raymond, suspecting that he was one of the Rebs who had fled from the house, raised his carbine and fired, and the man fell.

Upon investigation it was found that he had been killed and that he was a brother of the young woman who lived at the house.

Corporal Raymond, when being praised by his comrades for his successful shot, did not seem at all elated, but much sobered to know that he had taken another's life. He seemed to be a man who was soldiering purely from a sense of duty and one whom the terrible scenes and excesses of war would never deprive of his humanity.

The Sergeant above referred to reported to the Captain, describing in graphic terms the attack on his advance guard and his masterly retreat. Great was the astonishment of the officers and men when they arrived an hour later and found the Corporal and his faithful comrades safe and sound with the balance of the Regiment.

One of the comrades who stood by the Corporal on this occasion was our present Secretary, Bart Griffin, and the other was Silas D. Case, who at Buckland Mills, October 19th, 1863, seeing a Lieutenant had lost his horse, dismounted and gave his horse to this Lieutenant. Case himself was captured and died on Belle Isle, at Richmond, Va., March 4th, 1864. He was one of the youngest and bravest in the Regiment. The combined ages of these three boys were less than 50 years.

1862.

ELLIOTT A. COOK,
Co. "C."
Dead.

Born October 15, 1830, at Oakfield, Genesee Co., N. Y.; enlisted at Tuscola, Mich., September 11, 1862, as Private in Co. "C," 7th Michigan Cavalry; was killed on the picket line at Robinson River, near Culpeper C. H., Va., October 8, 1863. Through the faithfulness and generosity of his companions his remains were sent to his old home in New York, and now lay across the road opposite where he was born. Report says he was ordered out on the picket line where he was killed, to take the place of someone who had been caught sleeping on his post. He lived about one and one-half hours after being shot, and was conscious to the last.

1863. 1901.

Oliver H. Perry,

Co. "C."

107 Wall St., Ionia, Mich.

Born at Flushing, Genesee County, Mich., December 8th, 1844; enlisted at Saginaw, Saginaw County, Mich., August 28th, 1862, as Private in Co. "C," 7th Michigan Cavalry; taken prisoner October 8th, 1863, at Utz Ford, Robinson River, Va., confined in Libby, Pemberton, Belle Isle, and Andersonville prisons; released at Baldwin, Florida, April 28th, 1865; mustered out at Camp Chase, Ohio, June 20th, 1865, and honorably discharged.

ARMY TRAFFIC.

By Oliver H. Perry.

It was a night of August, in 1863, that two comrades, Walter Honsinger and William Hunter (I think) and myself were doing picket duty on the Rappahannock River at Bank's Ford. Our post was close to the river. Behind three small logs we laid all night with nothing to disturb our vigil until just at daylight when looking across the river in the gray light of morning we saw three Johnnies standing on the other side, their muskets sticking in the ground, a sign that hostilities were suspended for the time being.

Upon making our appearance one of their number said, "Hello, Yanks, you'ns got any coffee and sugar to trade for tobacco?" We told them we had, and if they would come over we would trade with them; but they insisted on our going across. After some little parleying Honsinger and I concluded it would be safe to make the venture, so after donning our bathing suits, "which consisted of the same outfit worn by Adam and Eve, minus the fig leaves," we started on what came very near being a dear expedition for us.

After going up stream some distance we started over, having with us our coffee and sugar. On arriving at our destination we did not go up onto the bank but sat down in the water to rest. After doing our trading and having a short talk with the Johnnies we concluded to return to our camp, when we were surprised to hear some one ask the guards who we'ns were. Upon looking up we saw a young Rebel Lieutenant standing there with all the dignity of a Corps Commander. Without asking us any questions regarding our business, or listening to any explanation he said, "You'ns get up and go to camp with me." About that time, if we had been on the other side of the river, we would have made them a present of our whole stock in trade, but there we were, breast deep in the water (to hide our bathing suits) and there seemed no other alternative but get out and go as prisoners to the camp of the "Johnnies," there to dry our suits and prepare for what was worse than death, Andersonville. Will God in His mercy draw the veil and let no record of that "Horror of Horrors" blot this history.

Excuse my digression; as we did not start at once he repeated his command, "You'ns get out and go to camp with me." Well, we thought it was all off with us, as we saw no other way than to go with him, when our friend of the tobacco deal, taking his gun from where it stood and covering his "superior," said, "Lieutenant, I told those men that if they came over they could go back, sir, and as I live I will keep my word with them, so now, 'Yanks,' you git and be right smart about it." Honsinger said, "He will shoot us," our friend said, "I guess not while he is interested with the close proximity of my musket."

Well, we accepted his invitation to "git" and were not long "gitting" either. I think the record for swimming was broken that morning, for the bubbles we made that went floating down stream were as big as canteens. Having plenty of salt, sugar, coffee and tobacco, we did not do as "Lot's wife" did, look back, but kept right on making suds. After we arrived on our side of the river we looked back and saw the Johnnies shoulder their arms and march away, and that was the last we saw of them.

How the matter was settled on the other side I never knew.

I have often wished I knew how fared our friend when he arrived at camp, but I am sure Providence cared for him. He was true to his word and showed a nature worthy of a nobler cause than the one he was contending for. If his life has been spared and if by chance or otherwise he should read this history, I wish to thank him for his honor as a man and his kindness to us, as I have had no opportunity to do so since we parted on that bright August morning in 1863.

1863. 1901.

WILLIAM HOOVER,

Co. "C."

Vassar, Mich.

Born in Jefferson County, N. Y., February 12th, 1843; enlisted at Tuscola, Tuscola County, Mich., August 30th, 1862, as Private in Co. "C," 7th Michigan Cavalry; mustered out at Fort Leavenworth, Kansas, December 15th, 1865, and honorably discharged.

1863.    1899.

REVEREND JOHN N. WILSON,
Co. "C."

Auburn, Ind.

Born November 19th, 1843, at Thetford, Genesee County, Mich.; enlisted at East Saginaw, Mich., August 31st, 1862, as Private in Co. "C," of the 7th Michigan Cavalry; mustered out at Annsville, Va., August 27th, 1863, the cause being heart trouble, and honorably discharged.

PASSING MOSBY'S PICKETS.
By Rev. John N. Wilson.

As the comrades are aware, in the early spring of 1863, the 7th Michigan Cavalry was divided into detachments, doing picket duty, patrolling, etc. As my memory has it, one detachment, consisting of Companies of which "C" was one, broke camp near Fairfax, April 10th, going to a point near Wolf Run Shoals, thence to Bristow Station and Cutletts Station, Warrenton Junction, Bealeton and Rappahannock, picketing the railroad and scouting and patrolling the country for Mosby's guerrillas, so that the boys in the 7th in my squadron knew the country well and nearly every point on the railroad from Fairfax Station to Rappahannock.

One fine day, about the first of June, we left camp at Warrenton Junction and leisurely made our way down the railroad to Rappahannock Station, going into camp about two o'clock.

About 5 p. m. Adjutant Doty came to me and asked if I would like to go to Fairfax—with dispatches—to which I eargerly said yes. He told me to report to headquarters at 6 p. m., which I accordingly did. Colonel Mann on being told I was selected to go to Fairfax questioned me closely about my knowledge of the road, my horse and arms. After apparently satisfying himself on those points he asked my Company, and then told me to go to Captain Darling and ask for ten men as an escort. I told him I did not want an escort of ten men, when he said then take twenty. I told him I wanted no escort, and on his insisting I told him that I had not been detailed for that duty, and if I was to go with an escort of ten or twenty men I would not go unless detailed for that duty. Upon his asking why I declined an escort, I told him one man well mounted, who knew the roads, could slip past Mosby and his men, when ten or twenty would be picked up or have to fight their way through.

The Colonel in response smiled and said, "You will do," and directed me to have my horse in readiness to start at 1 a. m., so that I might go through the worst part of the territory before daylight.

Leaving headquarters at 1 in the morning, a bright starlight night, with my big envelope with dispatches safely buttoned inside my jacket, I sallied out.

As you, my comrades, will remember, there were picket posts, or rather camps composed of one hundred or more men, strung all along the line of railroad to protect it from being destroyed by the Rebels. Each of these had their own countersign, and my instructions were, when hailed, to answer, "Friend, without the countersign," telling who I was and adding "with dispatches." So answering, I would be told to dismount and come into camp—when I would be taken to their headquarters, my papers, which were unsealed, examined, and I put in charge of a guard, who passed me out on the other side of their picket line.

I had passed two or three such posts and was within some two miles of Warrenton Junction, with my horse on a walk, when he swerved towards the railroad track, which at this place was four to six rods distant, and in a cut of four to six feet in depth. Reining him back into the road, and glancing that way to see what had caused him to act as he did, I was surprised, and I think I can safely say, "badly scared" as well, to see a man sitting quietly on his horse just across the track from me, and in the woods about forty rods away a dozen or more smoldering camp fires, with now and then a brand breaking, sending up sparks and flaring into a blaze. Having passed over the road that day and knowing we had no force of troops there, I at once concluded that it was Mosby or some of his men, and my carbine was hastily drawn from its socket and firmly grasped for immediate use. My intentions were, if hailed by him, to answer by a shot from my carbine and try to run to Warrenton Junction, or if too closely pushed take to the woods when I reached a strip closing in on both sides of the road about half a mile ahead. Holding my horse to its walk, I could see the silent horseman turn his head and watch me, as long as I could see him without turning. About forty rods further on the woods came down to the railroad on his side, and near this corner sat another horseman watching, I keeping the same gait, passed this picket, who in turn seemed to watch me, at the same slow gait walked on my way, until the shadaws of the woods covered me, when by use of spurs my horse was put to his best gait till Warrenton Junction was reached. To say I was scared is to speak mildly, I am not sure but that my hair stood on end.

On reaching headquarters of the infantry post at the Junction, I told the officer of the day what I had seen, who at once sent out orders for doubling up of pickets and to be in readiness for a dash by Mosby. Pushing on, Cutlett Station was reached and its officers notified of Mosby being near at hand, as also at Kettle Run and Bristow Station. At each of these places I was urged by the officers to remain till day, but declined.

Just as I struck over the ridge between Bristow and Manassas Junction, the sun rose. Passing Manassas Junction and the old Rebel camp, I crossed Bull Run at Blackburn's Ford and was taken to headquarters at Union Mills when, after the usual examination of my papers, I was placed in charge of a Corporal and passed out towards Fairfax. Every mile or so I would come to a picket post, by whom I would be stopped and the Sergeant or Lieutenant in charge of the line would interrogate me, look at my papers and pass me on, only to have the same thing repeated at the next post, and so on until I reached Fairfax and made my way to camp and turned over my papers in safety to General Copeland, our Brigade Commander.

I afterward learned that within one half hour from the time I reached Warrenton Junction, Mosby's force came, but finding the pickets alert and ready for them swung around and in turn tried the posts at Cutlett Station, Kettle Run and Bristow. Reaching the latter point shortly after I left the camp but in consequence of my warnings the pickets were not surprised and that raid was in vain.

1901.

CHARLES HUSTLER,

Co. "C."

Tuscola, Mich.

Born at Lewiston, Niagara County, N. Y., May 22nd, 1845; enlisted at Saginaw, Saginaw County, Mich., September 20th, 1862, as Private in Co. "C," 7th Michigan Cavalry; wounded at Greenwich, Va., May 29th, 1863, by gunshot in right thigh; taken prisoner at Trevilian's Station, June 11th. 1864, and taken to Richmond, Andersonville, Millen, then to Savannah, and paroled March 26th, 1865; mustered out at Clarksville, Md., June 30th, 1865, and honorably discharged.

1901.

ERNEST VON DANIELS,

Co. "C."

787 West Lake St., Chicago, Ill.

Born in Germany, October 6th, 1844; enlisted at East Saginaw, Saginaw County, Mich., November 29th, 1862, as private in Co. "C," 7th Michigan Cavalry; mustered out at Fort Leavenworth, Kansas, December 15th, 1865, and honorably discharged.

LEFT ON PICKET.

By Ernest Von Daniels.

We were camped at the ford of a small stream near Kettle Run. Bryant Rudd and myself were detailed by Acting Sergeant Wm. Glover Gage to guard the road leading to the ford. I remember that it was a warm, bright, sunny day, and we were right in our glory in being assigned to the post that we were. There were no Rebs in our immediate vicinity, everything was quiet, and it was just one of those balmy Southern days that makes a man fall in love with nature.

We were stationed about a mile from camp, doing duty until noon, and then began to look for relief, but none came. We ate some of the "grub" that we had in our haversacks and continued waiting for the relief. Evening came; we were getting tired; still no relief and no sounds from camp. We began to wonder. We ate supper from what we had left from dinner, watered our horses and began to argue with one another as to what was the best mode of procedure. Rudd was for going to camp to find out what was the matter while I stayed on guard, but I convinced him that that would be deserting his post, so he stayed.

We did duty that night, all the next day, the next night, and just before daybreak we heard a noise across the river. It sounded like the tramping of horses, and pretty soon we could see in the dim light a company of Cavalry approaching from the other side. We waited until they got about to the water's edge and then called out our challenge, "Who goes there?" "Friends, with the countersign," came the answer. We did not know whether they were Rebs or our own men, so we advanced and called, "Advance one and give the countersign." They wanted us to come half way, and then came the question of argument. I wanted Rudd to go, and Rudd wanted me to go. We argued, and finally Rudd convinced me that I, being the youngest, should go; so I went. I did not have the countersign, so I had to bluff it out. I met their man in midstream, and was just about tickled to death to find that he was from the 25th New York Cavalry.

Their Colonel ordered us to fall in with his Regiment and they would proceed under our guidance to the place where we thought our camp would be. When we got there, I'll be "swangogled" if the whole darned shootin' match hadn't moved and left us out there on guard.

We stayed with the 25th until their Colonel had found out where our Regiment had gone, then we were told to go and join them, which we did.

I would like some time to get a chance to put Comrade Gage on guard at a small ford in a lonely neighborhood. I'd leave him for a week and then send a troop of Sioux Indians to march on him and frighten him as badly as we were frightened that night. We thought the 25th was Mosby's men, and visions of Libby and Andersonville prisons stared us in the face from every side, and I assure you I was more pleased to find that they were a New York Regiment than I would be if I found a gold mine in my back yard to-day.

1864.

JAMES L. ROCK,

Co. "C,"

87 Fitzhugh St., Rochester, N. Y.

Born at Greece, Monroe County, N. Y., March 18th, 1835; enlisted at Corunna, Mich., February 27th, 1864, as Private in Co. "C," 7th Michigan Cavalry; mustered out at Salt Lake City, Utah, November 30th, 1865, and honorably discharged.

1901.

JAMES L. ROCK,

FORAGING AROUND TREVILIAN'S STATION.

By Jas. L. Rock.

During the campaigns of 1864 and 1865 many exciting events in battle and on the march occurred under my observation, but I will confine myself to the Battle of Trevilian's Station, which occurred on June 11th and 12th, 1864.

While on the march our rations became scarce and on the day before arriving at Trevilian, details were made throughout the Regiment to go out and collect rations and forage for the command. I was one among those detailed from Co "C" (in all about 15 men), among the number I distinctly remember Von Daniels, Honsinger, and Darby. Of the list of houses visited that day was one having the appearance from the exterior and surrounding grounds that the owner was a person of wealth. A short distance from the house on the south side were six or seven negro huts, in front of the west side was a beautiful lawn extending about 400 feet to the road running north and south. It was decorated with beautiful flowers planted in beds, artistically laid out, presenting a picturesque view from the house to the road. On arriving at the premises, pickets were stationed around the house, the balance proceeded to investigate, first by soliciting forage and rations for the Army from the inmates of the house, consisting of an old man and a young woman. Their reply was that there was not anything to meet our demands in or around the premises. Not believing them, we demanded the keys of the house and outbuildings, which demand was complied with and we proceeded to search for rations and forage. After making a thorough search we could not find anything and were disappointed and about to leave when our attention was called to the fact that there must be a garret above the floor which we had visited. We found a square hatch in the ceiling and in order to reach it one man had to climb on another's shoulders. The hatch was opened and on inspection we found bacon and meal enough to supply the Potomac Army one entire day. The joyful news was soon communicated to the other boys and our Commissary Pro Tem commenced firing out the bacon through the front window, every side going kerchunk right into a choice bed of flowers, it being located directly under the window. The young woman on seeing the bacon flying through the window and her flowers crushed, commenced a tirade and called us everything but gentlemen. She commenced by saying that the lowest Confederate could not, and would not, get so low as to commit the deed we were then enacting. No, they would die in the ditch with starvation first; they were gentlemen, every one of them, and we were not; that we were not men of principle, only Lincoln's hirelings, gathered from all over the world, composed of robbers, thugs, gamblers, mudsills, and murderers, hired to destroy their homes. All the time that she was raving we, of course, were packing the bacon on our saddles and smiling. As no one would answer her epithets she became more enraged and paced the verandah from end to end, her hair loosening and falling down her back. Finally in her exaspiration she called us dummies and hoped the Confederate Army would have the pleasure of eating the bacon we were taking, and prayed God that she might live to see the day and that the opportunity might arise giving her the chance to eat a Yankee scalp. Little did we think at that time that one of her wishes would be fulfilled, and that, too, on the very next morning, for as we were making coffee and cooking flap-jacks the Rebels fired into our midst and we immediately vacated, leaving them the whole of the bacon that we had captured the day before. Getting out into the open and the light of day approaching, the first sound that greeted our ears was a Michigan yell, coming from the throats of the gallant old 1st. They made a successful charge, bringing back about 300 prisoners, army wagons, ambulances, etc.; then a charge was made by the 5th, then the 6th, then went in the invincible 7th, it being about 7 a. m., and stayed in until the engagement for the day ended. All members of the 7th remember that engagement, as it was "cut and slash," we being outnumbered four to one, forced us to charge and fight in small detachments, charging back and forth over the same ground three or four times before relief came by our fighting through and making connections with the balance of the Corps. One interesting incident came under my observation that day, I happening to get alongside of General Custer in one of the charges just as his color bearer was shot; he dismounted, tore the colors from the staff, and remounted. He advanced but a short distance when he met the Captain of Battery "M," who stated that he had just lost one section of his Battery and pointed in the direction that it was taken. The General put spurs to his horse and was out of sight in a few seconds and that was the last I saw of him that day, as I had plenty of business to engage my attention from that time to the finish. I speak of this eventful day as a subject for thought, after hearing the expressions and sentiments of the cultured lady of the South whom we met the day before. If her sentiment prevailed throughout the rank and file of the Southern army and citizens, we can without being considered egotistic feel proud of being a fractional part of our great army of men that opened the door and let in the light of intelligence and happiness to our once sectional enemies, but now our best friends, and as such may we always remain.

1865.   1886.

ALBERT M. HELMER,

Co. "C."

Parma, Jackson Co., Mich.

Born November 27, 1846, at Lockport, N. Y.; enlisted at Jackson, Mich., as Private in Co. "C," 7th Michigan Cavalry, February 15, 1865; mustered out at Fort Leavenworth, Kan., December 15, 1865, and honorably discharged.

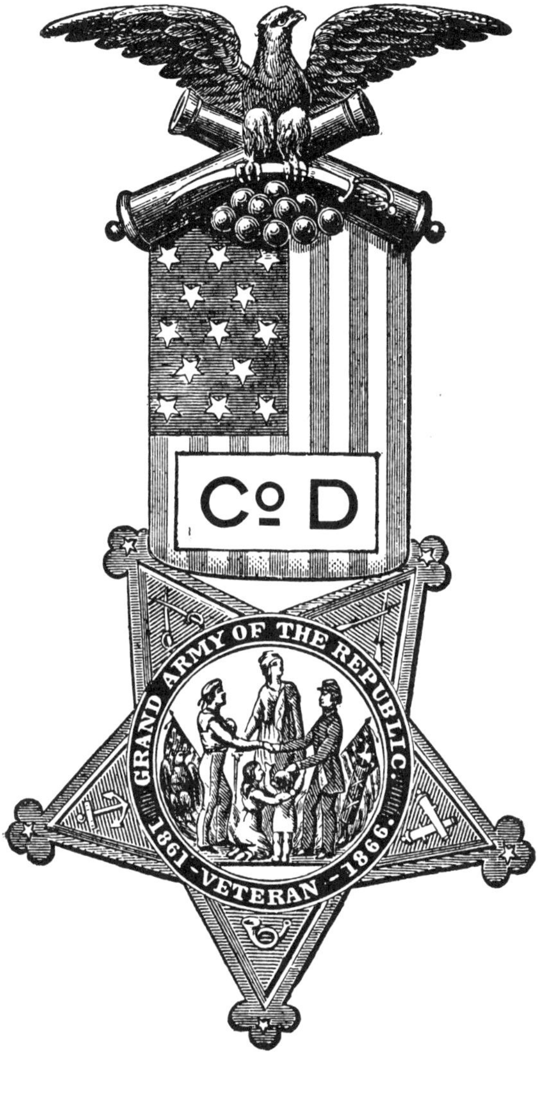
Co D
GRAND ARMY OF THE REPUBLIC
1861 - VETERAN - 1866.

1863.   1901.

George A. Armstrong,

Captain Co. "D."

1034 P. St., Fresno, Cal.

Born at Peru, Clinton County, N. Y., August 27th, 1830; mustered at Grand Rapids, Kent County, Mich., November 13th, 1862, as Captain of Co. "D," 7th Michigan Cavalry; promoted to Captain and A. Q. M. May 24th, 1864, and served as such until the close of the war at Nashville, Bridgeport, and Knoxville; wounded July 16th, 1863, being thrown from a horse and landing on my head, which nearly broke my neck, taken up for dead and left at a farm house. November 26th, 1863, was appointed Aide to General Stoneman at Washington, later was dismissed from the service and tried by Military Court, was reinstated and appointed Captain and A. Q. M.; honorably discharged at Washington, D. C., March 13th, 1866.

AT THE BATTLE OF GETTYSBURG.

By Capt. Geo. A. Armstrong.

On the second day of the Battle of Gettysburg the 7th Michigan Cavalry had been for some time supporting a Battery that was playing vigorously upon the enemy, who were returning a lively fire, and we listening to the zip, zip of their bullets as they passed, as well as the boom of some hundreds of cannon and the screeching of shells. A good looking young officer rode out toward us, waving his hand, and in a pleasant tone of voice called out, "Bring on your 7th now," and the Regiment in column of companies moved out in order to strike the column that was trying to turn our flank, first at a slow trot, then at a double quick, then the charge. We went over the hill at a break-neck charge, down into the pit-hole of death into a corner of a stone wall with a fence on top of it; Colonel Mann was in command, General Custer riding near him at the head of the command. We crashed against the stone wall, which withstood us, breaking our columns into jelly and mixing us up like a mass of pulp. "Throw down the fence!" was ordered, and the rails flew in all directions, clearing an opening for us to pass, while the Rebels with their guns poked through the fence as they lay securely behind the wall were raking our helpless column with their deadly fire. Through the gap in the fence our brave boys went pell-mell, their horses jumping the wall and at them we went every man for himself. Young Wm. H. Adams of my Company fell almost into my arms shot dead as his horse leaped the wall. The enemy recoiled and withdrew only as we cut or shot them down or rode over them. We withdrew and reformed our broken ranks and shattered companies, charging them again, going over the wall the second time, cutting, slashing and shooting them down, but they were too heavy and sullen for us and stood their ground so desperately that as before we were compelled to withdraw over the wall a second time, badly broken and cut up, and as we were trying to reform a Rebel Regiment of Cavalry swung into view, charging down upon us. I rode up to General Custer and called his attention to their advance, he answered, "Yes, I know it, and we must get back under the guns," but at that moment the 1st Vermont Cavalry charged over the hill to our rescue. On they came, both Regiments, the Rebels and the Vermonters coming together like two furious thunder clouds, and then occurred a wonder of the battle field, every soldier held his breath and his heart stood still for the moment; when within easy pistol shot both Regiments halted for a moment, faced each other, looked each other in the eyes, then a yell rang out from the 1st Vermont and they spurred their horses forward in a desperate charge, the Rebels wheeled, were driven off the field and out of sight.

Henry Thomas, Private of my Company, later Lieutenant, had two horses shot under him and came off the field all O. K. on the third horse that he picked up. Such was much of the desperate fighting in the three days fight at Gettysburg.

1862.   1869.

JAMES G. BIRNEY,

Captain Co. "D."

Dead.

Born at New Haven, New Haven County, Conn., August 12th, 1844; enlisted at Bay City, Mich., September 10th, 1862, as Private in Co. "C," 7th Michigan Cavalry; was promoted to Second Lieutenant of Co. "C" October 15th, 1862; to First Lieutenant August 1st, 1863, by order of Colonel W. D. Mann, "in reward for brave and noble conduct on the bloody field of Gettysburg, where in gallant defense of our colors he was struck down and taken prisoner;" and assigned to Co. "A," and to Captain March 18th, 1864; wounded and left for dead on the field of Gettysburg, taken prisoner July 3rd, 1863, escaping two nights after; transferred to 1st Michigan Veteran Cavalry November 17th, 1865; mustered out at

Salt Lake City March 10th, 1866, and honorably discharged.

Entered the Regular Army as Second Lieutenant, 9th United States Cavalry July 23rd, 1866, "was Breveted First Lieutenant and Captain March 2nd, 1867, for gallant and meritorious service at the Battle of Gettysburg; promoted to First Lieutenant April 14th, 1867; died at Fort Davis, Western Texas, January 16th, 1870.

EXTRACT FROM A LETTER OF LIEUT. JAMES G. BIRNEY.

On the day of the great Battle of Gettysburg (Friday), we had a very sharp fight with General Stuart on the right. The 7th Michigan Cavalry charged gallantly and drove them back; when Hampton's entire Brigade charged us, and we were obliged to fall back. My horse was shot twice and finally killed; a bullet went through the pommel of my saddle, two through my overcoat and one through my sabre strap, and I was struck on the heel with a spent one. The Regiment began to fall back and just then the Color Sergeant (Church, of Bay City) was killed by a pistol shot. I secured the colors and was charged on by a large number of Rebels, and I can assure you the bullets whistled merrily for a while, but miraculously none touched me. I shot two of the enemy, using all the charges left in my revolver and then charged a man with the pike of the colors, but before I reached him I got a sabre cut on the head that laid me out. I lay upon the field for an hour when the Rebels came and carried me off, a prisoner. I was a prisoner for two days, one of which was the Fourth of July. I escaped from them above Cashtown and found Uncle Fitzhugh of the Ambulance Corps, who took me in his ambulance to Middletown, where I found General Pleasanton's headquarters and reported for duty with a request to be forwarded to my Regiment. The General was very complimentary and appointed me as Aide-de-Camp on his Staff.

DEATH OF A GALLANT OFFICER.

Captain James G. Birney, eldest son of Hon. James Birney, of Bay City, Mich., died January 16th, 1870, at Fort Davis, Texas.

Captain Birney, after serving four years in the Volunteer Service under Generals Custer, Kilpatrick, and Sheridan, received an appointment from Secretary Stanton in the 9th Cavalry of the Regular Army, and was on duty at Fort Davis when he died.

Major-General Hatch paid the following tribute in a letter communicating the sad intelligence of his death:

"Captain James G. Birney died this morning at five o'clock. The Captain had complained of a serious indisposition for some time prior to January 2nd, when his illness confined him to his bed. From that time he sank rapidly under a severe attack of acute inflammation of the stomach that resisted every effort of an accomplished army surgeon. God willed he should pass gently away, dying so easily in the presence of his wife and brother officers he seemed to have fallen into a quiet sleep. I need not say how thoroughly he was loved by his brother officers. The qualities that endeared him to them must have been delightfully prominent in the home circle. He had every attribute of manhood. To a face and form unusually excellent was connected ability and energy sufficient for any purpose directed by the highest integrity, combining the finest qualities of an officer and a gentleman. His endurance and courage in the field were wonderful."

1864   1893

J. Q. A. SESSIONS,

First Lieutenant Co. "D."

911 Forest Ave., Ann Arbor, Mich.

Born January 15th, 1832, at Lenox, Madison County, N. Y.; received First Lieutenant Commission from Austin Blair (Governor) October 15th, 1862, and was mustered in 7th Michigan Cavalry as First Lieutenant in Co. "D," November 13th, 1862; was with my Regiment in Battles of Gettysburg, Hanover, Boonsboro, Culpeper, Morton's Ford, Brandy Station and Kilpatrick's Raid to Richmond. A Rebel bullet went through and knocked off my hat at Gettysburg and my horse was hit by a Rebel bullet at Battle of Morton's Ford, but no wounds for me; mustered out at Fort Leavenworth, Kan., November 3rd, 1865, and honorably discharged.

REMINISCENCES OF THE PICKET LINE.

By Lieut. J. Q. A. Sessions.

My first experience in charge of a picket line was on the Chantilly Pike soon after our Brigade went into our first camp in Virginia, at Fairfax Court House, in March or April, 1863. One dark night I concluded to ascertain how reliable the pickets were to prevent unknown persons from passing the posts on the Pike without first giving the countersign. We were picketing against Mosby's guerillas and instructed to give an alarm if they attempted to make a raid inside our lines. I commenced my trip on my horse down the Pike at the west end of our line near Centerville, going eastward. Pulling my hat down over my eyes, my coat collar turned up, I soon approached the first picket. "Who comes there?" Changing my voice to as gruff a tone as possible, I replied, "A farmer living near Fairfax; I have been to Centerville and want to get home." "Advance. Have you the countersign?" "I know nothing about countersigns, but want to get home. Can't I pass down the Pike?" "Yes, you may pass. I guess you are all right." The same thing occurred with variations at two other picket posts, except I was questioned more closely as to what I had been to Centerville for, etc. Of course I had been on business and detained later than I had expected. On my route I had met a Corporal or Sergeant of Co. "D" and explained the trip and requested him to go with me.

When we approached the fourth post, where the boys had built a large fire out of logs, we were halted at some distance from the picket, probably as soon as we were heard coming. "Who comes there?" "Two farmers who have been to Centerville on business and want to get home; we live near Fairfax." "Dismount one and advance." I crawled off my horse as clumsily as possible and led my horse towards the picket. I heard the click of the revolver as I had at one or two other posts. I realized that in the hands of men of so little experience the revolver was liable to go off and I might be sorry I undertook the trip. By the time I had approached near this picket, another man had come out from the fire near the post and I was confronted by two of them.

With my hat drawn down and stooping over, they could not see my face. After several questions and answers, one said in a low tone to the other, "Lead him up to the fire!" Of course I had to go. He stooped down and looked up into my face. "My God, Lieutenant, is that you?" A shout from the boys and the fun for me was over.

I once had charge of the picket line on the north bank of the Rappahannock a few miles above Fredericksburg. About noon I visited the picket line. At the headquarters of the pickets who were in charge of a Sergeant, the boys were getting dinner. There was hard tack, coffee, fried bacon, and I think a loaf of bread, which must have come down from the skies like manna to the wandering Israelites.

Across the river sat two Rebel pickets on horses in the shade of a tree. "Boys," said I, "suppose we invite the pickets on the other side to come over and eat dinner with us." "Oh, they won't dare to leave their posts and come over here." "Well, I am going to see what they will say about it." "Hello!" One replied, "Hello!" "We are getting dinner, come over and eat with us," giving him at the same time the bill of fare. "I will see you back all right." "Oh, no, we can't, the officer may come around here soon." "There is no danger of that, he is looking after his own dinner now."

"I can't swim," said one. "Can the other swim?" "I can swim some, but wouldn't dare try it alone." "Will you come over if I will swim across and escort you?" After consulting together he said, "Yes, I will try it." "Well, meet me at the bank. I will be there." He met me at the bank prepared for a swim and we passed over all right. Throwing a blanket around him, and giving him a hard tack box for a seat beside another box used for a table, he said, "By golly, this seems queer, don't it?" "What is the matter?" "Why, we are eating dinner together to-day and perhaps shooting at each other to-morrow." "Well," I replied, "it is to-day now, let to-morrow take care of itself." He said he was eighteen years old and was raised near Richmond and that he had not had any coffee for six months, and that it was the best dinner he had received in a long time. I went back with him and though the current was rapid, nothing occurred to mar the festive occasion. Several years afterwards it occurred to me that this was one of the most indiscreet and foolish acts of my life. If he had lost courage in the middle of the stream and seized hold of me, I was not strong enough to hold him up and keep him at arm's length, and both would have gone to the bottom, and remained there for an indefinite period.

In October, 1863, General Lee advanced on our Army from his headquarters in and around Gordonsville, the Union Army being in the vicinity of Culpeper. Our Brigade (Custer's) and other Cavalry covered the retreat, protecting the wagon trains. We marched toward Washington as far as Bull Run, and Centerville. On October 14th, 1863, a portion of both armies collided at Bristo Station, a railroad station west of Bull Run. Here the Rebels got the worst of it and lost two Regiments, taken prisoners, besides many killed and wounded. Portions of our Army crossed the Run over the little bridge made famous by the first and second battles of Bull Run in '61 and '62. Our Brigade went into camp near the bridge. About dark my Company ("D") was ordered to go a mile west where the second battle of Bull Run was fought, form a picket line through the woods and remain during the night. It was too dark to distinguish skulls from stones, or dead bodies shriveled in their clothing or partly covered with earth, from sticks of wood. At daylight we had a view of a battle field, a year after the battle occurred, where thousands were slaughtered. I hope I shall never see such a sight again.

We were in a Charnal House of immense proportions. Our Army was defeated and retreated to Chantilly. But little time could be spared by either army for burying the dead. This was evident from appearances. In several places trenches from twenty to forty feet long and twelve to eighteen inches deep were filled with bodies. A little earth and tufts of grass were placed over them. Imagine the situation a year afterwards. The day previous it seemed quite certain there would be a third battle of Bull Run. But that night and the next day General Lee retraced his steps and went back with his entire army to his old camping grounds in and around Gordonsville. Our Army followed and occupied our former positions. The Cavalry leading the way.

In the fall of 1863, after the armies under Lee and Meade had settled down again in permanent quarters, our Regiment was sent to the Rappahannock opposite Fredericksburg on a reconnoisance to ascertain, if possible, what General Lee was doing or what he proposed to do after his ruinous defeat at Gettysburg. Soon after we arrived at the river it was reported that the Rebels on the opposite side had been sending over Southern papers to one of our Regiments, who had camped there a short time previous. A very small boat, with a very delicate rudder and a paper sail was sent across the river, with the bottom of the boat filled with papers. The rudder was set and fastened in such a way that the boat would be driven across the river by the current and the paper sail. On further inquiry we learned the boat went down stream the day before. I proposed to Captain James B. Loomis, now living in Nome, Alaska (then Sergeant-Major of the Regiment), that we swim across, get some of the papers and bring them back in our hats, provided the Rebels on the other side were good natured and would agree to see us back all right. I said, "Hello, there, have you any papers?" "Yes, come over and get some." "Can't you send them over?" "No, we have no way now." "If two of us come over will you see us back all right?" "Yes, come, on, we will see you back all right, and give you some Richmond papers." At the same time raising both hands, to indicate "no arms," and that they would receive us bare handed. This was a promise and signal along the Rappahannock so long as it was the boundary line between the two Armies. Many a meeting of the pickets to exchange papers and Yankee coffee for Virginia tobacco was arranged in this way and not a single instance was known where either party broke his word. It was considered a matter of honor on all such occasions. Loomis said he did not think he could swim across, the current was so strong. I said I was going directly over. Loomis went up stream a short distance and swam and floated across diagonally. I swam to a large rock on the bank. The Rebels, including some bright looking officers, seeing us coming, had flocked to the shore.

As I crawled up on the rock one of them asked, "Are you a Yankee?" "Well," I said, "my parents were born in New England, I was born in New York State, and I hail from Michigan. You may call me what you choose." "Well, who is General Meade?" The calamity of Gettysburg was still fresh in their minds. I replied, "He seems to be a man whom the Lord has raised up to put down this Rebellion." "Oh, he can't do that, we can carry on the war twenty years yet." One said they could carry on a guerilla war, if necessary, for twenty years. I replied that long before the twenty years were passed they would find it did not pay and would get tired of it. This was merely good natured banter, no hostile feeling being manifested by any one. "Well," said I, "where are the papers.

I think we must be going back." "All right, bring down some papers," said an officer. We placed the papers in our hats, bade them good bye and swam back to the northern shore. Our anxiety to get Rebel papers was caused by the bombardment of Fort Sumter by our forces. Our batteries there were knocking the fort into a big heap of rubbish and the Rebels received the news several days earlier than we did.

1863.   1900.
ALBERT SHOTWELL,
Q. M. Sergeant Co. "D."
Dimondale, Mich.

Born in Elba, Genesee County, N. Y., January 16th, 1840; enlisted in Windsor Township, Eaton County, Michigan, September 12th, 1862, as Corporal in Co. "D," 7th Michigan Cavalry; promoted to Sergeant August 15th, 1863, and to Q. M. Sergeant December 31st, 1864; mustered out at Fort Leavenworth, Kansas, December 15th, 1865, and honorably discharged.

WINCHESTER.
By Albert Shotwell.

One day's experience during my army life which impressed me more than any other was the 19th day of September, 1864, known as the Battle of Opequon Creek or Winchester.

We broke camp about 2:30 o'clock that morning and started to cross the creek. Our Regiment was to support the 25th New York Cavalry, which we did in fine style, the 25th going down to the Ford and taking a road to the right, the 7th following, which brought us back to nearly where we started from; the two Regiments making a grand appearance. Afterward the 7th took the lead and crossed the Ford, where we found the Johnnies in full force. Shortly after we made a charge on their earthworks and met with a warm reception and stubborn resistance, but we carried the works and won the day by routing the Rebels in great style. In this charge one of our boys had his horse disabled by his fore legs being shot off. Peter B. Palmanteer took leg bail for some bushes, the boys cheering him with "go it, Pete." However, Pete got there all right.

We followed the Rebels toward Winchester, skirmishing all the way until we found them in force. Our Regiment was ordered to charge them, which we did and drove them some distance, when all at once we came along by the side of a stone wall, running parallel with the way we were going, behind which the Rebels were. They rose up and gave us a volley in our left flank, which was a surprise and stirred us up in great shape. The first I knew there were only three of us left, Colonel Brewer, Comrade Christian Bush of Co. "D" and myself. I was carrying the Regimental colors for Colonel Brewer, who said, "Sergeant, we better get out of here or we will lose the colors." Just about this time my horse was shot in the flank and Christian Bush was shot and killed. His foot caught in the stirrup and he was dragged back until the boys caught his horse.

The grandest sight I saw during my army life was on this day. Sometime in the afternoon we were drawn up for another charge, our position being on the right of our line next to the Infantry. We were on high ground and could see the

Infantry charging toward Winchester. Next comes the order to us; we hear the bugle sound, which is the signal for us to charge, away we go over a little knoll, and we are in the midst of the Rebel Infantry who are waiting for us, formed in a hollow square; we do not stop nor slacken our charge, but ride right through and over them, taking most of them prisoners. During this charge the Rebels had a battery planted so it threw shells into our ranks from the right front. One shell hit my horse in the head, and in falling he threw me, colors and all, quite a number of feet over his head; I immediately caught another horse, mounted and had just overtaken the Colonel near a large building on the left when occurred one of the saddest calamities of the war to me—our brave Colonel Brewer was shot and mortally wounded.

The day was won, we had routed the enemy and cleaned them out completely. We now felt the need of rest and went into camp. Thus ended one of the most eventful days of my army life.

1866. 1901.

ANDREW PRAY,

Sergeant Co. "D."

Dimondale, Mich.

Born January 4th, 1845, in Superior Township, Washtenaw County, Mich.; enlisted at Grand Rapids, Mich., November 12th, 1862, as Private in Co. "D," 7th Michigan Cavalry; promoted to Corporal in 1863, and to Sergeant in 1864; taken prisoner March 2nd, 1864, on Kilpatrick's Raid, escaped the same night of capture; mustered out at Fort Leavenworth, Kansas, October 28th, 1865, and honorably discharged.

Remarks: On the 10th day of November, 1862, in company with C. H. Holmes and William Bell, I left Windsor Township for Kalamo to enlist under George McCormick.

On arriving there we found that McCormick had gone to Grand Rapids. Holmes and I then started on foot for Grand Rapids, getting as far as Portland the first day. The next morning we took the stage to Lyons and from there took the cars on the D., G. H. & M. R. R., arriving at Grand Rapids in the evening; enrolled our names in Co. "D," 7th Michigan Cavalry, and were mustered into the U. S. service on the 13th day of November, 1862. I think I walked much farther to enlist than I would have done one year later.

ON KILPATRICK'S RAID TO RICHMOND.

By Andrew Pray.

The night of March 2nd, 1864, after the first attack by the Confederates, while on the Kilpatrick Raid to Richmond, Lieutenant Sessions sent me with four men to the left and across a road along a fence at the edge of a clearing to hold them back on that side of camp. We had not been there long when I heard firing in our rear and suggested to the boys that we had better get out of there and make a run for camp. In the woods where our horses were we could see men about our camp fires and supposed they were our men until we were right among them, and they invited us to surrender. There were three Rebs hitched to me, one hold of each arm, and the third had hold of my coat in front. The one in front unbuckled my sabre belt and he and the one that had hold of my right arm began quarreling over my revolver and let go of me. I had my carbine on my shoulder and I raised it up with my right hand over my head, when the Johnnie that still had hold of me said, "You have a gun, too, have you?" and let go of me. I said, "Yes, sir," and turned and ran for where I supposed my Regiment was. The three with some others took after me, hollering "Halt!" Seeing a line of skirmishers at the lower edge of our camp, I thought they were our men until I was within two rods of them, when one of those following me shouted, "There goes a Yankee, shoot him." Then I saw what I was up against, but was too frightened to stop. The skirmishers, even facing the same way I was running, and I ran between two of the Rebs, who cut loose at me. I was running down the hill and they firing high was all that saved me that time. After I got to the bottom of the hill and away from the light of the camp fires and in the timber I saw the reflection of water in a ditch. I gave a leap for the other side, struck a grape vine with my head and went back into the ditch casouse, sitting down in the water nearly up to my shoulders. I crawled out on my hands and knees and found it was an old fence row with a road running along near it. I took to the middle of the road —ran about half a mile and caught up with the rear guard of our command. From there on for about three miles I was putting in my best efforts, part of the time I was head of our rear guard and part of the time between the two lines. The roads were a muddy slush and I got so tired out that I would stub my toe and fall full length in the mud. I finally got a lead horse from a darky and rode it until I caught up with my Regiment, which had gone into camp. I was so played out when I got to camp that I laid down by the first fire I came to. I had lost everything I had to wear or cover up with, as all I had left was pants, boots and jacket. When daylight came and we were ordered to move I was so sore and lame I could not move myself. The boys of my company picked me up and put me onto a stray horse they had caught and without saddle or bridle, having only a halter, I rode through to Yorktown. When the command went into camp the boys would take me off the horse and when they moved again they would load me on again. I absolutely had no use of my legs. The associations of such times and the hardships passed together and endured are what makes us comrades to-day.

AT APPOMATTOX.
By Andrew Pray.

Early on the morning of April 9th, 1865, when we started on the advance there were just five of Co. "D" present for duty, four Sergeants and one Corporal. The Corporal held the horses and the Sergeants went to the front to fight on foot. We drove the Rebel skirmishers back over a long hill and the four of us then stopped in the point of a flat-iron shaped piece of timber and lay in fence corners surrounding it. The Rebel lines began to advance and we were so busily engaged trying to keep them out of our neck of the woods that we did not notice they were getting around to our left and rear and into the woods. The first we knew the woods was full of them. They commenced firing at us from the flank, then we began to look for the rest of our skirmish line, but they were all gone, so we struck out across an open field to our right and rear. It was about half a mile back to the top of the hill and running up hill was not easy work for a dismounted Cavalryman. The Rebel skirmish line that was in front of us was advancing and those in the woods pecking at us from our right, but running up hill was helping us out, as they were all shooting low. The minnie balls and gravel were flying around our feet and as Charlie Holmes said as he and I were making our best time side by side, "Sandy, this makes a fellow pick up his feet mighty quick, don't it." George Ferris and Al. Shotwell were better on foot or had better wind than Holmes and I, for they reached the top of the hill first, but they did not have to wait long for us. When we got to the top of the hill we saw our Infantry coming out of the woods. We moved over towards them out of range of the Rebel line that came to the top of the hill, but when they saw our Infantry advancing, turned about and went back. We waited until our Infantry came up when we went back to the top of the hill with them. Shotwell and I retired to the shade of a tree to rest, thinking we would see an Infantry battle. Ferris and Holmes went back with the skirmishers to get a little revenge for the run they had given them, but we were all disappointed, as the skirmishers had not reached the foot of the hill when the flag of truce came out and there was a happy time along the whole line. We then went over to our right to our command and horses.

1864.

William H. Pollard,

Co. "D."

Charlotte, Eaton Co., Mich.

Born July 7th, 1834, at Penzance, Cornwall County, England; enlisted at Charlotte, Mich., October 6th, 1862, as Private in Co. "D," 7th Michigan Cavalry; mustered out at Fort Leavenworth, Kansas, December 15th, 1865, and honorably discharged.

KILPATRICK'S RAID AROUND RICHMOND.
By William H. Pollard.

About sundown on the evening of the 28th of February, 1864, we left Stevensburg on a forced march, I in command of Headquarters' wagon; everything went well, we did not halt or stop until about noon on the 29th, when the General decided that we would take a lunch, but when we looked into the wagon there were no eatables there. During the night I had taken in two dismounted men to give them a lift and they had taken all there was to eat and drink and skipped. "I think they belonged to the 6th Michigan Cavalry." I do not think any of the men of the 7th Michigan would have done so mean a trick. As there was nothing to eat we stopped but a short time and about two o'clock that night we went into camp. Not knowing how long we were to remain, I thought I would improve whatever time there was and take a nap, which I did. Had only slept a short time when I woke up and found the fires all out and headquarters gone, leaving me behind. I was at a loss to know what to do, as it was a very dark, uncomfortable and disagreeable night and dangerous to be left behind and alone, so concluded the safest thing to do was to start my mules and get out, but did not know which way to go. I finally decided to direct my course toward a fire I saw in the distance, which on reaching proved to be a fire left by some of the column that had already passed by. Unfortunately, there was a ditch between me and the fire well filled with water and on account of the darkness I missed the bridge that crossed it and the first thing I knew my saddle mule and myself went over the bank into the water. My position was very uncomfortable and critical, as I feared every moment the Johnnies would put in an appearance. The only chance I saw for my relief and release was to unload the wagon, which I did, then the mules were able to get us out. Making a circuit I came around and struck the bridge all right and soon got near the fire that I saw.

The officer of the rear guard halted me to know what was coming. I answered, "The General's wagon." He said I was just in time, and getting in ahead of them I felt all right once more. I followed in the wake of the column and about noon got inside of the second line of fortifications. There was a splendid park and several nice houses around in it. At this point a negro appeared, having driven out from the city on his way for his Missus. He had a splendid carriage and two played out mules. He informed me that he came out after his Missus every week, she being out here to visit her daughter; said he did not expect we-uns all up there that morning, if he had he would have stayed back in the city. Two sick officers took possession of the rig and started on their way to Yorktown. My mules were tired and hungry, so I decided to do some foraging in order to replace the ten sacks of oats that I left back in the ditch. I found plenty of corn and also some nice chickens in a hen-house. There were four ladies at the residence; they did not raise many objections to my entering the coop; I think there must have been from four to five hundred as nice chickens as I ever saw, and eggs without number, I judged they had not gathered them for a day or two. I did not go very heavy on the pullets, took five nice ones and what eggs I could stow away and left the rest for some of the other boys. We soon started on the advance, moved to the right and continued our march until about ten o'clock, when we went into camp. Our advance was surprised and routed and a great number went by headquarters on a double quick, this continued for some time when the General ordered his horse and mounted. He continued in the saddle and waited sometime, apparently for his staff to report, but as they did not put in an appearance he concluded to get out and told me to come; I did not want the second invitation. He and I, I think, were the only two in the yard where our camp was. After a march of a mile or so I overtook the General, where a line had been formed, and we then moved in column for about three miles and again went into camp. As we had not had any chance to make coffee I concluded to make some and cook my pullets. Having a large camp kettle I concluded to cook the whole of them, so got them ready and had them nicely boiling when an officer of our Regiment came and asked me if I had anything to eat. He said he presumed he was like all the rest of the command, very hungry. Pretty soon he espied the pot and smelled the chickens and wanted to know if that was mine; I told him it was. He did not wait for an invitation, but got his knife and fork and began operations, remarking that he preferred his chicken rare and said the trouble with the boys was they cooked them too much. After he had been eating some time he said if I had no objections he would go over and get the rest of his mess and we would all have a good square meal. I of course acquiesced with his request, but when we were through there was very little left. We soon continued our march and overtook the officers who took the darkey's rig, which they drove until the mules played out, when they left the carriage by the side of the road and I took it in tow and hauled it through to Yorktown, where the General made the Commander of the Fort a present of it.

So ended our Raid to Richmond.

1862.   1902.

GEO. W. DOBSON,
Co. "D."
Litchfield, Mich.

Born at Stainton, Durham County, England, September 12th, 1843; enlisted at Kalamo, Eaton County, Mich., September 1st, 1862, as Private in Co. "D," 7th Michigan Cavalry; was wounded by having a horse fall on me the first day of March, 1864, near Richmond, Va.; taken prisoner the second day of March, 1864, served part of the time at Belle Isle and the other part in Hospital; paroled April 16th, 1864, and joined Regiment July 20th, 1864; mustered out at Fort Leavenworth, Kansas, December 15th, 1865, and honorably discharged.

WITH GENERALS SHERIDAN AND CUSTER. OCT. 19, 1864.
By George W. Dobson.

The evening of October 18th, 1864, I and a detail were with Captain Jas. G. Birney at Winchester, Va., with new men and horses for the front from Dismounted Camp at Harper's Ferry. As I was a friend of Captain Birney I tented with him. On the morning of October 19th, 1864, we heard the roar of guns in the direction of Cedar Creek, which was twenty miles away. I reported what I had heard to Captain Birney as we rode over to General Sheridan's Headquarters, and as he was desirous of going to the front, he detailed a Sergeant to take command of the men and horses; he and I then went to the front with General Sheridan. I shall never forget that ride; how we met men of the 8th Corps in their shirts and drawers and in a general demoralized condition. On the way General Sheridan said, "We are going back to our old camps to-night." When General Custer met General Sheridan on the field he saluted him with these words, "Looks as though we are gone up to-day." General Sheridan said, "The right will prevail." Custer replied, "We will go back to our old camps to-night or I will sacrifice every man in my division, and I will go with them." Those who were there know that we did go back to our old camp. If we had had two hours more of sun not a Rebel would have gotten out of that valley.

1863. 1878.

FRANK MILBOURN,

Co. "D."

Potterville, Eaton Co., Mich.

Born in London, England, May 3, 1848; enlisted at Charlotte, Eaton County, Mich., January 23, 1863, as Private in Co. "D," 7th Michigan Cavalry; wounded at Gettysburg, July 3, 1863, in the stomach; taken prisoner at Gettysburg, July 3, 1863, at four o'clock, and escaped at ten o'clock that night; mustered out at Washington, D. C., November 23rd, 1865, and honorably discharged.

EXCITING RECOLLECTIONS.

By Frank Milbourn.

I was with the Regiment from the time it left the State until August, after the Battle of Gettysburg, when I was taken sick with typhoid fever at Falmouth, Va., and was sent to Washington, D. C. When General Custer took command of our Brigade I was detailed as his Orderly; was with him when he led our old Regiment in the charge on the last day of the three days' fight at Gettysburg.

Was taken prisoner about four p. m. on the 3rd of July, the Rebs took me about six miles with about 50 of our boys, including George Mason of my Company, who afterwards died in Andersonville. The Rebs gave me my supper, it was flour, but looked more like mill sweepings. I asked them how I should fix it so I could eat it; they told me to mix it up with water and eat it, that was good enough for a d—— Yankee, but I did not. They formed a guard around us at dark; along in the evening they passed through our guard line with heavy artillery, and as one piece passed near me I got on a cannon and rode out. It being dark they did not notice me and I escaped and returned to my Regiment. I thanked God they did not see me. George Mason could have gotten away with me if he had had a mind to, but he feared he would be killed. The Regiment that captured me was the 5th Georgia Infantry.

On the night of July 4th, myself and Lieutenant Littlefield, of Custer's Staff, located the enemy's train and our Command captured it.

At Falling Waters I was with 70 of our Regiment who captured 400 prisoners, I taking five of them to the rear; on the way one of them, an officer, tried to get a pistol from out his pocket to shoot me, but I saw him in time to disarm him, which probably saved my life.

1895.

ALBERT H. OLMSTEAD,

Co. "D."

St. Louis, Mich.

Born October 15th, 1845, at Windsor, Eaton County, Mich.; enlisted at Charlotte, Eaton County, Mich., September 9th, 1864, as Private in Co. "D," 7th Michigan Cavalry; mustered out at Detroit, Mich., August 16th, 1865, and honorably discharged.

1901.

EDWIN O. RUSSELL,
Co. "D."

Grand Ledge, Mich.

Born at Portland, Ionia Co., Mich., March 16th, 1844; enlisted at Grand Ledge, Eaton County, Mich., January 24th, 1865, as private in Co. "D," 7th Michigan Cavalry; commissioned as Recruiting Officer by Governor Blair, March 20th, 1864; mustered out at Fort Leavenworth, Kansas, December 15th, 1865, and honorably discharged.

WATCHING FOR J. WILKES BOOTH.
By Edwin O. Russell.

At "Belle Island Ford," on the Potomac, a few miles below "Point of Rocks," Md., in the Spring of 1865, Sergeant John F. Simpson, of Co. "M," with some twelve or fifteen men were guarding this Ford. On the day after the assassination of

President Lincoln, about 2 o'clock in the afternoon, an officer came riding down the towpath, his horse on the dead run and covered with foam. Halting in front of our tent he called for Sergeant Simpson and told us of the assassination. He said Booth with a body guard of thirty men were making for our Ford and ordered extra precautions to be taken to intercept and capture him "dead or alive." I was one of those detailed to patrol the towpath from our post to the next above. A dense fog soon set in and night came on dark and gloomy, so dark that it was impossible to see the brass buttons on our dark blue coats. I had made one trip over my beat and was slowly feeling my way along about midway of my second when a heavy plunge in the canal surprised and startled me. My cap rose clear off my head, invisible fingers pullel at every hair, my nerves grew suddenly tense, and my first thought was, "Here they come—fire! quick!—give the alarm!" A second impulse said, "No, wait a moment," all of which went humming through my brain with lightning speed. Booth is here, what should I do; what would one of the "old boys" do. Keep cool, my boy, you are a recruit. Don't fire yet; be sure before you give the alarm. How fast thoughts came and crowded each other. I could hear loud rippling of the water in the canal; they were surely crossing, right here. Pulling myself together with an effort, I raised the hammer of my carbine, pulling the trigger at the same time to prevent loud clicking of the lock, stepped quickly down the bank toward the river, dropped on one knee, held my carbine ready to fire, and waited. How long it seemed, and how dark—if I could only see. The strain was terrible. I was breathing hard and thinking fast of what would occur when they came out on the towpath. Fire—give the alarm—and then jump farther down the bank toward the river when their shots would go over me; dodge about among some trees and stay there until the "boys" came, even if I were killed for it. Something scrambled noisily out of the canal; I sprang to my feet; it came straight towards me with a bound and a shake that threw sprays of water all around and over me, and my scare was over. I dropped the butt of my carbine on the towpath as a large Newfoundland dog put his forepaws almost on my shoulders. The dog belonged to a negro family near by. I was weak and trembling, but was proud to think that I had not given a false alarm.

This experience gave me confidence in myself during the balance of my service, whether on picket or other duty, while crossing the plains, or on the mountains among hostile Indians of the then far West. However, the incident was not reported to Sergeant Simpson until thirty years later.

1901.

CORYDON CROSSETT,
Co. "D."

27. N. Jefferson St., Battle Creek, Mich.

Born at Clarendon, Orleans County, N. Y., February 28th, 1833; made application to muster as a U. S. soldier May 15th, 1861, was refused owing to undersize; enlisted at Battle Creek, Mich., February 21st, 1865; mustered at Jackson, Mich., March 1st, 1865, in Co. "D," 7th Michigan Volunteer Cavalry; joined my Regiment at Harper's Ferry, Va., on active duty and remained with them through the campaign of the West; mustered out at Salt Lake City, Utah, March 10th, 1866, and honorably discharged.

1865   1900

JUDGE GEORGE P. COBB,

Co. "D."

Bay City, Mich.

Born at York, Livingston County, N. Y., April 13th, 1841; enlisted at Ann Arbor, Washtenaw County, Mich., March 17th, 1865, as Private in Co. "D," 7th Michigan Cavalry; mustered out at Camp Douglas, Utah, February 21st, 1866, and honorably discharged.

REMINISCENCES.
By Geo. P. Cobb.

One who joined the service during the last year of the war can perhaps say little that will interest the veterans, or add zest to what has been said by them; and it is with great diffidence that I have complied with our President's request for reminiscences. Although identified for some time with the grand old 7th Michigan Cavalry I can say nothing from personal knowledge of its battles and campaigns in the South.

A wish to be "in it" had followed me from the first, resolutions to get in had been thwarted and I had finally settled down to the belief that I was to have no part in the business. Early in 1865 there was another loud call for recruits, it seemed as though the final struggle was at hand, and I dropped everything, incurring losses that will never be repaid, offered myself as a soldier and was accepted.

A few days later my squad was at Fort Federal Hill, Baltimore, Md., from whence a steamer conveyed us to City Point, Va., being two nights on the route. We had practically nothing to eat or drink; the fault was supposed to be that of the officer in command, "not a Michigan man," and the things that were said about him and to him could have led to a court martial. The second night, owing to the crowded and filthy condition of the deck, I did not lie down, but stood at a little window staring at the rain, thick darkness and flashes of artillery outside.

After our arrival and having been duly counted, delivered and receipted for, we, in company with a thousand other soldiers and exchanged prisoners, were entertained for a week at the military hotel called the "bull pen." The mud was not very deep and our water barrels were replenished almost every day from the river. Then our squad was transferred to a remount camp two or three miles down the river, where we sometimes heard firing and hourly expected an order to take a hand (which order never came).

At that time the Custer Brigade was pretty well scattered. The main body was at the front not far away. A detachment was at Pleasant Valley, Md., and in our camp at "City Point" was another large detachment; also with us about 2,000 other dismounted Cavalrymen. The camp was under command of Colonel Anderson, a Pennsylvanian. Whenever we could get a few horses, men were sent to their Regiments. It so happened, without any solicitation or suggestion of mine, that my duties kept me almost continually at headquarters; at first in the Quartermaster's department and afterwards in the Adjutant's. At that camp I made the acquaintance of many commissioned and enlisted men for whom I formed a high regard, but most of whom I have not seen since 1866. The Michigan detachment was commanded by Major Darling, Lieutenant Gray of the 5th Michigan Cavalry acting as his Adjutant. On duty in the camp were Lieutenants Canfield and Havens, Captains Sergeant and McCormick of the 7th, Captain Rockafellow of the 6th, and Captain Berdan and Lieutenant White, all good men and true, and I must not forget old Dr. Upjohn. From the first I heard him roundly abused and denounced as a butcher, but my own acquaintance, which began when I was desperately sick, left me with feelings of the highest respect and good will for him as a kindly, generous old man.

One night there was riot in the camp. Three large sutler's tents disappeared with their contents as if by magic. Bullets were buzzing around like bees. Colonel Anderson's adjutant found it convenient to leave the camp that night and he was never seen there again. One man went to hospital, seriously wounded.

Late in May, "just too late for the Grand Review," there was a trip to Washington by steamer, thence to Parkersburg, W. Va., by rail, another boat excursion to St. Louis, Mo., and then to Fort Leavenworth, Kan. Up to this time I had belonged to the 5th, but while I was wandering around looking for that Regiment, Captain Sergeant met and informed me that I had been transferred to Co. "B" of the 7th, and kindly went with me to my Company and introduced me to the First Sergeant, George A. Hart, also just transferred from the 5th, who then and there detailed me for clerical work.

A week there and then the long march across the plains. There was much that was tedious but little that was exciting, excepting on one occasion when we were fording Platte River, when Colonel Briggs missed the trail and he and horse suddenly disappeared. We feared that some big fish had caught the horse by the foot and pulled him under, but they soon appeared on the surface, found the trail again and the excitement subsided.

July 28th found us at Camp Collins, where, I think, three Companies, "H," "L," and one other, remained. My Company ("B") going further West, but at the last moment an order came for me to remain and report to Lieutenant Dunnett. I found that Dunnett had been detailed as Adjutant of the post and wanted me as his clerk. Colonel Briggs made Camp Collins his headquarters and whenever he was absent Major Warner was the senior officer. Captain Clipperton was there and on one occasion when there was a burial service to be read and no Chaplain to read it or book to read it from, he made himself useful by reciting the service complete, from memory. Some little awkwardness of the firing squad moved him to throw in some expressions not found in the prayer-book and he made them load and fire again.

The Paymaster had forgotten us and we were in need of money. Prices were soaring in the clouds. Money sent from home seldom reached its owner. Something had to be done. The corn furnished to feed our horses could be sold for ten dollars a bushel. One day Colonel Briggs accidentally found himself in a position to hear a conversation just around a corner and out of his sight, in which Billy Fisher, Co. "H," was negotiating the sale of a bushel of corn to a citizen. The Colonel held his breath until he was sure the ten dollars had changed hands, when he appeared before the men, revolver in hand and ordered the citizen to drop the bag and run. He then marched to his office the very picture of offended military dignity, and directed his orderly to summon Mr. Fisher before him without delay. Billy came. Whether the Colonel tied him up by the thumbs or bucked and gagged him or devised some other cruel form of torture was never told, but in a few minutes Billy returned to his quarters looking happy and contented and nothing more was heard of the affair.

During the ten weeks at Camp Collins an event that produced the greatest sensation and sorrow was the capture, torture and murder of Corporal George Baker, of Co. "B," by Indians, near Little Laramie, by tying him to his wagon and burning him alive.

In October a portion of our Regiment pushed on Westward. Snowed in one day at Rock Creek. Camped a few days on Pass Creek among droves of antelope and flocks of wild ducks. Was poisoned for a week with the villainous waters of Bitter Creek. Half frozen on the bluffs of Green River, and finally camped near Fort Bridger for three weeks. Here occurred the reorganization, or consolidation, by which the remnants of the 1st, 5th, 6th and 7th became one full Regiment, under the name of 1st Michigan Veteran Cavalry. Four Companies were left at Fort Bridger and the others marched to the Salt Lake Valley, taking possession of Camp Douglas near Salt Lake City. The Paymaster had not come yet and the boys were hungry for something better than army rations. Many of them had plenty of Confederate scrip. The farmers of the Valley knew nothing about paper money and were intensely ignorant generally. They invaded the camp with their wagons loaded with vegetables and fruit, going away with pockets full of bills, leaving behind considerable silver change. But that did not last long.

The garrison was made up of Michigan and Nevada Cavalry and Artillery from California, all a lot of "Galvanized Yankees." Each had its own organization and all reported to Colonel Potter, commanding the post. He was a good man, or meant to be, but his West Point training had made something of a martinet of him and he could not appreciate the feelings of volunteers who had served to the end of the war and long afterwards and wanted to go home. He had plenty of trouble and deserved part of it.

Just after our arrival there was a grand review of all the troops and as it seemed to me chiefly remarkable for the displayed awkwardness.

Commissary supplies were necessarily expensive. The Government had stored in an immense wooden building about $1,000,000 worth. During the night of December 18th, 1865, it was found to be on fire. Everybody turned out and a bucket brigade was organized and did what could be done, but much property was destroyed and all were more or less injured. Early the next morning a court of inquiry was convened to examine witnesses to find out how the fire originated, and it continued in session until midnight. Lieutenant Dunnett, then in command of Co. "B," predicted that we would all be hungry before spring, but before daylight General Conner's Quartermaster had contracted for a large amount of supplies in the city and our rations never failed.

January 1st, 1866, a general court martial convened and it had not finished its work when I left the camp on February 21. I did all the clerical work for these two courts and one other, while practically doing all the work of the Adjutant's office. After Colonel Briggs left, Captain Birney had command of the Michigan detachment. His Adjutant was Lieutenant Frank

B. Clark, then only twenty years of age. During four years of hard service, Lieutenant Clark had not been wounded, but soon after his discharge, while on the homeward trip, he stumbled and fell over a tent rope and was killed by the discharge of his own revolver.

I have mentioned many of our commissioned officers, but I also remember many brave, big-hearted men who, although they never wore shoulder straps, were excellent soldiers and men, and worthy of all praise. At this moment the names occurring to me are Sergeant George A. Hart, Co. "B;" Sergeant Marshall Bellinger, Co. "A;" Sergeant Al. McLouth, Co. "B;" Sergeant Crane, Co. "E;" Robert J. Kelley, Co. "F;" George House, Walter E. Bush, Otto Feyeraben, John Paul, Co. "I."

Co E

GRAND ARMY OF THE REPUBLIC
1861 · VETERAN · 1866

1864

1900

ROSWELL HARTLEY HOLMES,
Captain Co. "E."
23 Joy St., Detroit, Mich.
Detroit, Mich.

Born at Holmesville, Oswego County, N. Y., November 25th, 1838; enlisted at Detroit, Michigan, August 10th, 1862, as Second Lieutenant in Co. "E," 7th Michigan Cavalry; promoted to First Lieutenant September 18th, 1863, on the field at Summerville Ford, Va., as per the following order, read to the Regiment at the close of the action:

"Second Lieutenant Roswell H. Holmes, Co. "E," 7th Michigan Cavalry, in reward for gallant conduct in the repulse of the foe in the late desperate attack on our lines, where he was most conspicuous in rallying back our forces, scattered and retiring before the vastly superior numbers of the enemy exultant over the defeat of the gallant 6th Michigan, and for efficiency is hereby promoted to be First Lieutenant, to rank as such from the first day of August, 1863. He will be respected and obeyed accordingly. Signed, W. D. Mann, Col."

Promoted to Captain for gallantry in action while in command of 2nd Battalion October 9th, 1863, when the 6th Michigan Cavalry was withdrawn and the 7th Michigan, under command of Colonel W. D. Mann, charged a Rebel force in front of Orange Court House, Va.; "not mustered as Captain;" taken prisoner at Buckland Mills, Va., October 19th, 1863, and escaped two days later by running Rebel guard; owing to ill-health resigned March 28th, 1864, and honorably discharged.

PERSONAL EXPERIENCE ON "KILPATRICK'S RAID TO RICHMOND—1864."

By Roswell H. Holmes.

The date was Sunday, the last of February, 1864, a bright, crisp winter's day. The place Stevensburg, near Culpeper, Va. Kilpatrick's Division, Cavalry Corps, Army of the Potomac, in winter quarters.

An Aide from the temporary Commander of Custer's Brigade rides swiftly down the front of the 7th—halts sharply at Colonel Litchfield's quarters and delivers an order. This order was: "Report your Regiment at General Kilpatrick's Headquarters promptly at sundown."

During the previous week, rumors had been rife of some impending movement. Orders had been given to each Regiment of the Division to select such officers, men and horses only as were fit for severe service, all missing equipments to be replaced, and extra horse shoes and nails provided. Consequently, the General's order to assemble occasioned no surprise, but much excitement and curiosity as to our destination.

In the absence of our Adjutant, who had gone to Michigan on important service, I was detailed to the duties of that officer, and at sundown moved the Regiment and reported it at the appointed place. Within an hour a force of about five thousand picked men and horses, including Pennington's and Elder's Batteries, five ambulances and five army wagons, with ample supplies of ammunition, powder and turpentine, moved swiftly to Ely's Ford on the Rapidan.

The 7th had the rear of the column and while crossing the river met the captured Confederate pickets, who had all been surprised and taken by the advance, and were now prisoners under guard going to the rear.

All night long with the 7th it was first a halt, then a horse race to keep closed up on the column. At early dawn on Monday, a brief halt—just long enough for the 7th to boil their coffee, but not to drink it. Into canteens it was hastily poured, while imperative orders were to "Mount" and forward again at a gallop. All day long and far into the second night there were the briefest halts—then "Forward, Trot"—or "Forward, Gallop." Past midnight we went into bivouac for a scant two hours—then a hurried "Mount" and forward again at a gallop into the darkness and the rain. Pushing on by obscure roads that wound through dense forests, morning found the outside men in each set of fours of the 7th nearly all bareheaded—for the limbs of trees bordering the road, weighted down by the rain, had brushed off the head covering of the men in their saddles on the march.

As the second day wore on, already many horses succumbed to the terrific strain of such a desperately forced march. When a trooper found that his steed would no longer respond to the spur, but would stagger with exhaustion, the unfortunate rider could only dismount, strip off his saddle and bridle, throw them on his shoulder, cling to the stirrup of some more lucky comrade, and hope for a mount. King Richard's "My kingdom for a horse" was trifling compared to the dismounted Cavalryman's offers for a like necessity. Women were met driving perhaps a single horse, or, better luck for our boys, a team; they were stopped, their horses unharnessed, saddled, mounted and in the column before the bewildered women could realize their misfortune. If horses or colts were seen in a field, they were instantly corralled and put into service.

Up to this time, the destination of this dashing and hazardous raid was known only to the Commanding General and his Staff Officers. Major Farnham Lyon was a Volunteer Quartermaster on Kilpatrick's Staff, and from him I learned that it was "On to Richmond;" our object, to make a dash into the city, liberate the prisoners in Libby and blow up and destroy what would most damage the Confederate Government. We also learned that in order to draw the attention of the enemy away from our movements and allow us to take Richmond by surprise, General Custer with a special force had gone to attack the Confederate Reserve Artillery and keep Fitzhugh Lee too busy to hinder our movements. Also that Colonel Ulrich Dahlgren, a brilliant Cavalry officer, son of Admiral Dahlgren, of the Navy, had been detached with five hundred Cavalry for the desperate duty of attacking Richmond from the south side, while we dashed in from the north; and a still farther part of the plan of operations was for General Benjamin F. Butler with a strong force of Infantry to join us after the attack and cover the retreat of Kilpatrick's exhausted command.

Before noon of Tuesday we struck the railroad, where we barely missed capturing General R. E. Lee, whose train was backed away in time to admit of his escape. Later in the afternoon we reached the immediate vicinity of Richmond. Passing through the outer line of unoccupied earthworks, we could see Kilpatrick with the 1st Brigade and the two Batteries, feeling the strength of the enemy at their second line of defense. At this moment the 7th Cavalry with the gallant and impetuous Colonel Litchfield in their front, stood in line with sabres drawn, ready for the General's order to "Charge." No signals had been received from Colonel Dahlgren that he was ready to attack on the south side and thus weaken the force opposing us, so General Kilpatrick decided to withdraw, which he did, towards Mechanicsville (six miles from Richmond) where, after placing pickets from the 7th the entire command went into bivouac. Late at night our pickets were driven in and our position shelled by forces under command of General Wade Hampton. The intrepid Litchfield himself led his Regiment to drive back the enemy and restore the picket line. In the mud and snow and dense darkness, with shells bursting among our men and among the horses hitched to trees in our bivouac, bravely fighting to hold his position, Colonel Litchfield, Captain Clark, Lieutenant Ingersoll, Sergeant David Genny and forty-four men of the 7th were captured.

Under cover of the dark and stormy night and the stubborn fighting of our men, General Kilpatrick with the main body of his command hastily retreated towards the Rappahannock. Unable to find any commanding officer to give orders or directions, I did what I could to gather our scattered companies together and finding the trail of the retreating column, we followed on through the night in much excusable disorder. Overtaking the main body of our expedition, we soon realized our crippled condition, and learned the extent of our losses in officers, men, horses and equipments.

Wednesday afternoon we reached White House Landing on the Pamunkey River, where we stopped to rest and feed the command. Here the remnant of Dahlgren's force rejoined us. I had placed pickets at a small stream some distance back on the route we had come. A challenge from our pickets to a force approaching from our rear revealed the fact that these were Dahlgren's men.

Here while we halted at White House Landing, I consulted the officers of the 7th and in view of the fact that we now had no Field or Staff Officers present for duty, I asked Colonel Preston, who commanded our Brigade, to detail Major Wells of the 1st Vermont to the command of the 7th, until our return to Stevensburg, which he did.

When General Kilpatrick resumed his retreat at sundown of Wednesday, we had been in the saddle all but sixteen hours out of the seventy-two since we started.

In my narration of this raid I am now nearing a point at which my personal knowledge of it comes to an end. Enfeebled by illness preceding this expedition, a serious accident together with exhaustion, now caused my collapse. And here I wish to pay tribute to a man who was always a good soldier and a brave, competent officer, whose modesty is only equaled by his valor. While halted near the Pamunkey River, I was laid on the ground, unconscious and in convulsions; Surgeon Richards was unable to secure any place for me in an ambbulance; a friend and comrade took the contents of my pockets and my sabre, gave them to Sergeant Major Carver to send home to my parents, and bidding his comrades good bye, let the command go on, while he remained with the unconscious body of his friend—to meet certain capture and probable death. "Greater love than this no man hath, that he lay down his life for his friend."

I deem myself derelict in my duty, that I have not sooner given this testimony to the heroism of your brave and modest comrade, Captain W. H. Fisher. It is your good fortune and mine that Comrade Captain Fisher is still with us, for, Kilpatrick finding the Pamunkey impassable, countermarched his columns and passing near Captain Fisher gave up his ambulance, in which I was carried to Yorktown and there placed in hospital by Surgeon Richards and Captain Fisher, to whom I owe the privilege of being able at this late day to tell the story of a great Raid and recount the perils and the heroism of the men and officers of the 7th, incident thereto.

1863   1895

George W. McCormick,

Captain Co. "E."

21 West 106th St., New York City.

Born in Ann Arbor, Washtenaw County, Mich., May 19th, 1838; enlisted at Kalamo, Eaton County, Mich., October 28th, 1862, as Private in Co. "D," 7th Michigan Cavalry; was promoted to Quartermaster-Sergeant November 29th, 1862, to Second Lieutenant June 6th, 1863, to First Lieutenant June 13th, 1863, and to Captain May 24th, 1865; was wounded at Rapidan River November 25th, 1863, being shot in neck; at White Post, "In the Valley," in right arm, face and body by sabre and shell; was taken prisoner at Buckland Mills, October 19th, 1863, and got away, again at Banks Ford, they let me go; was mustered out at Fort Leavenworth, Kan., December 15th, 1865, muster out countermanded, final discharge November 11th, 1869, at Washington, D. C., and honorably discharged.

REMINISCENCES.
By Captain George W. McCormick.

When we look back nearly forty years and try to remember things that took place then it is difficult to write about the Civil War and the part the grand "Old 7th" Michigan Cavalry took in it from 1863 to 1865. If all could be written it would fill volumes and no one person could do it justice.

What more glory can a man want than to be able to say that he was a member of the 7th Michigan Cavalry which, no doubt, saw as many battles and skirmishes as any Regiment in the Union Army. A few of the battles, commencing with Gettysburg, July 3rd, fighting all day and night, going through the mountain pass to Hagerstown; 6th, hard fight at the latter place; 8th, at Boonsboro and Williamsport; 9th, another fight at Hagerstown; 14th, at Falling Waters, next Amosville, Culpepper, James City, Jack's Shop, Hawe's Shop, Brandy Station, Morton Ford, Raccoon Ford, Groveton, Wilderness, Spottsylvania, Beaver Dam Station, and, by the way, the first shot fired at Spottsylvania was at a detachment of the 7th; then came Yellow Tavern, where we lost poor Major Granger; then Mechanicsville, Old Church, Coal Harbor, Malvern Hill, Trevilian Station, and, by the way, I think that the hardest battle of the War for the number of men engaged; then Meadow Bridge, Kilpatrick's Raid and the Grant Campaign, commencing May 4th, 1864. When we crossed Mine Run there was not one day for over a month that the Regiment was not under fire, and I often think of a remark a recruit made who had joined us just before we started on this campaign; he said, "Soldiering was not such a d—n soft thing after all, fighting at 40 cents a day, when he could get 75 cents a day at home hoeing corn." He was in dead earnest; from what he had seen he supposed we began fighting every morning regular, the same as a man worked on a farm. Then came our troubles on the James River and around Petersburg and Black Water.

For a long time it had been running in my mind that I would have to do something or I would be ordered before a military commission. You see, unfortunately, I happened to be born "Irish," and to cap the climax was red-headed, and I knew something had to be done to bring me up to the standard, so I got all the money together I could raise and bought me a trunk and filled it with fine clothes; they were the pride of my life, and no wonder, they were the first that I had ever had and I was sure when I put them on my time with the "Old 7th" would be short, and to tell the truth that was the reason I delayed day after day. Of course I had to tell someone of the great surprise I was going to spring on the boys; all remember an honest kind of a fellow who was known by the name of Sproul; I think he studied some time or other for the ministry. I told him my secret; he said it was a good thing, but that it would be sure to make more or less trouble, as every commanding officer would want me on his staff, but we finally decided that it would work out all right, as I would likely be called to Washington on some special service; those clothes were the idol of my eyes. Sproul wanted me to let him wear them, but I would not; you may think it was selfish in me not to loan them to him, but at that time he and Major Warner were quarrelling and they sometimes would use knives, and I was afraid my clothes might be ruined. While we were marching along the James River I discovered a fine fishing place out on a point and decided to try it as soon as we got into camp; without waiting for supper I started for the point. I found it a hard place to get to on account of tangled vines, brush and dry creeks, which we crossed on poles, Lieutenant Knight being with me. We had not been there long when water began running into my boots over the tops; we looked for land and there was none in sight, so we started for camp. We labored all night, the dry creeks we crossed in going had plenty of water in them when we came back. We got to camp just in time to hear "Boots and Saddles," and everyone, except a small guard, were ready to start on a raid to Black Water, we having no time to change our clothes or get anything to eat. We were gone a number of days, had a hard trip, came back ragged and covered with the soldiers' pests; but there was one happy man in the crowd, for I had decided that this was my time. I would throw away all my old clothes, get a bath and shave, put on my new suit and be the envy of all. What a change is sometimes brought about in a short space of time; when we got back to camp we found that Mosby had been there, carried off nearly everything we had, cut the lock out of my trunk, "it being sole leather," leaving nothing but one paper collar. Can you blame me for being pleased when we were ordered to take transports to a point near Washington, as Early was getting disagreeably near the Capital?

Then came the campaign of the Shenandoah Valley. We met Early in force, first, at Sheppardstown, then Smithfield, where we lost Lieutenant Mead; then Front Royal, where Lieutenant Carver was killed; then Winchester, where Major Brewer was killed. After Winchester I was away until about the first of January, having been wounded the day Carver was killed; on my return I was on a raid with Colonel Maxwell, who had 500 men of the 1st Michigan, and it proved one of the most exciting of all my experiences during the War.

The 25th day of February, 1865, we broke camp near Winchester and started up the valley, and it proved to be one of the greatest campaigns of the War. At Gainsboro poor old Early saw the last of his army and left them without ever saying "Good-bye," very unsoldier-like. There was hard marching through the mud and many will remember when General Devens was in command of our division that we had been marching every night until 12 and 1 o'clock; one evening just at dark the column halted at the side of a beautiful piece of woods with plenty of rails; there we stood to horse until near morning, when it was discovered that Devens was sound asleep on his horse. Of course there was some swear words uttered.

After the War the papers had a great deal to say about the French Tobacco that was burned near Stanton. If they would give anything worth while I could tell them of our work on the railroad and canal around Charlottsville. I think it was as fine and complete as I ever saw.

Then followed our drawing near to Petersburg, which point we had left nearly a year before, and where we were to see the end of the great struggle, far the greatest the world has ever known; the "Old 7th" was at the taking of Petersburg and at the surrender of General Lee, and always did her full share, never shirking any duty.

Why should not a man feel proud to say he was a member of the 7th Michigan Cavalry, and I believe there was more harmony among both officers and men than any other Regiment in the service, and as the time goes on that comradship grows stronger.

After the surrender of Lee and our good and hard service, we had the promise, and I think all supposed we would be the first troops to be mustered out, but instead we were sent west to fight Indians. At the time most of us were very much disgusted, but like good soldiers as they proved themselves they submitted with good grace and very little grumbling, and at this time I presume the majority are glad that they made the trip, as now they have a much better idea of this glorious country of ours which we risked our lives to save.

With the "Old 7th" is closely allied the 1st Cavalry. I can see them to-day as plain as I did on July 3rd, 1863, when under that brave officer, Colonel Town, they charged and helped us out at Gettysburg. The 5th and 6th each claim to have lost more men than any other Regiment in the Michigan Brigade; be that as it may, they saw no more active fighting nor served their country more faithfully than the "Old 7th."

Since the War I have often been asked if I ever saw a dead Cavalryman, they saying they never had. I always said "Yes," then asked them what branch of the service they were in; they invariably said "Infantry." I tell them no wonder; to see dead Cavalrymen they had to go to the front; if they had ever got there they would have found plenty of them.

1864   1899

ALBERT CRANE,
First Sergeant Co. "E."
121 N. Prospect St., Grand Rapids, Mich.

Born in Penn Yan, Yates County, N. Y., February 1st, 1841; enlisted at Ypsilanti, Washtenaw County, Mich., September 5th, 1862, as private in Co. "E," 7th Michigan Cavalry; was promoted to Corporal January 23rd, 1863; to Commissary Sergeant October 1st, 1863, and to First Sergeant June 24th, 1865; was in the engagements of Port Royal, Jack's Shop, James City, Brandy Station, Buckland Mills, Morgan's Ford, Richmond Raid, Mechanicsville, The Wilderness, Yellow Tavern, Old Church, Coal Harbor, Trevilian's Station, Smithfield, Cedar Creek, Dinwiddie Court House, Five Forks, Sailors' Creek, and Appomattox; also in two Indian fights with Sioux Indians, on the upper waters of Cache La Poudre and Laramie Creek; mustered out at Fort Leavenworth, Kan., December 18th, 1865, and honorably discharged.

1900.

WALDEN W. RAYMOND,
Sergeant Co. "E."
Williamston, Mich.

Born October 27th, 1840, at Dexter, Washtenaw County, Mich.; enlisted at Wheatfield, Ingham County, Mich., September 10th, 1862, as private in Co. "E," 7th Michigan Cavalry; was promoted to Corporal December, 1862, and to Sergeant February, 1863; was mustered out at Fort Leavenworth, Kan., November 9th, 1865, and was honorably discharged.

REMINISCENCE.
By W. W. Raymond.

I had the distinction of being the first member of the Regiment to down a Rebel, which took place at the Marstella Farm, eight miles north of Warrenton Junction, Va., on a reconnoitre led by Colonel W. D. Mann with about forty men of his Regiment, on the 14th of May, 1863.

At Gettysburg on the 3rd of July, in the excitement of the hour and through the carelessness of the Rebels in our front, my horse was shot just as we were ordered to fall back; through fear and foolishness I remained there. The Rebels advanced and passed me, I playing possum to keep from being taken prisoner until our men drove them back and let me out. Being dismounted I walked to Frederick City, Md., where I procured another horse and joined the Regiment on the 10th of July. On the 14th this horse was shot twice while making a charge at Falling Waters, Md.

One of the most important events of my soldier life took place on the 14th August, 1864, at Middletown, Shenandoah Valley, Va. It was the execution of a spy captured by Custer's Command the day before, I being appointed scaffold builder and chief executioner of the day, not a very desirable position. I have forgotten the victim's name.

I sumbit this as a bit of uncolored history of my soldier life, although there was enough excitement from start to finish to keep one from having the blues, and write volumes, but not enough to keep one from wanting to return home to follow and enjoy the peaceful pursuits of a law abiding citizen.

1862.   1900.

DAVID G. GENNY,

Sergeant ,Co. "E."

Detroit, Mich.

Born in France, February 12th, 1842; emigrated with my parents to America in 1854; enlisted at Southfield, Oakland County, Mich., September 20th, 1862, as Private in Co. "E," 7th Michigan Cavalry; promoted to Corporal in November, 1862, Sergeant July, 1865; taken prisoner March 1st, 1864, confined in Pemberton, Belle Isle and Libby prisons, paroled August 11th, 1864, joined Regiment in December, 1864; mustered out at Fort Leavenworth, Kansas, December 15th, 1865, and honorably discharged.

KILPATRICK'S RAID IN 1864.
By David G. Genney.

The "breaking" of camp and crossing of the Rapidan River in the dead of night, on Sunday, February 28th, 1864; the forty-hour gallop around Lee's Army to within the outer fortifications of the redoubtable Rebel Capital, arriving about two o'clock Tuesday afternoon; the shelling of the place by our "Flying" Artillery against the Johnnies' heavy siege guns; the repulse and abandonment of the project of the capturing of the Rebel stronghold with 5,000 men; the jaded condition of our horses and the final retreat of a few miles and quietly going into camp in a piece of woods right in the heart of the Southern Confederacy, is a story still fresh in the minds of all who took part in that dare-devil attempt, and has been told and retold by abler tongue and more graphic pen than mine; hence it is not my purpose in this brief sketch to give a detailed account of that daring and somewhat Quixotic expedition other than that which relates to myself.

As soon as we went into camp and I had secured my jaded horse to a sapling and built a camp fire, I was intent on procuring some kind of provender for him. I followed the usual line of camp foragers, which led to a barn in which there were some corn stalks, and while groping in the darkness in this building, "a darker night even Tam O'Shanter never saw," I heard three shots fired in close proximity to the barn and a man yell "Murder!" There were others who heard the ominous sounds, as there was an immediate exodus from that building and a silent hustling back to camp. I had just arrived at Co. "E's" quarters and while engaged in the care of my horse, feeding it some of the fodder, a sudden rattle of musketry broke upon the misty night air. It was evident that the reserve picket post had been attacked and that we had active business on our hands with at least one-half of the men fast asleep. I distinctly heard Col. Litchfield command, "This way, dismounted men." I having a "Burnside" single shot carbine, called to Comrade C. Y. McClain to loan me his long Seven-Shooter "Spencer." After securing it and with pockets full of cartridges, my tent mate, Corporal Daily, and I proceeded as best we could in the impenetrable darkness toward the sound of the Colonel's voice, and finally reached the edge of the woods and what appeared to be an open field, where the Rebs had a battery of four guns. History says two, but I know from the flashes of the guns that there were four with which the Johnnies were pouring shots into the woods. I think this battery was not twenty rods from the providential ditch in which we were lying and using our Spencers as rapidly as we could work the levers, firing towards the flashes of the guns. It was rather an unequal duel, but Daily, who was quite a wit and would crack a joke in the very face of a cannon, declared we had silenced their battery, at least they quit firing and we returned to camp. Arriving there we found nothing but smouldering fires and some dead horses; hearing a body of Cavalry moving along the road we walked in that direction and right into one of Wade Hampton's North Carolina Regiments. I should very much like to have seen my jocular comrade's expression of countenance after having blandly asked the very natural and usual question on such occasions, "What Regiment is this?" and receiving as an answer the cold muzzle of a carbine pressed to the side of his head with the pre-emptory command, "Throw up your hands, Yank." I know I was a decidedly mild and meek "Yank" on the receipt of similar treatment by them. On the principle that misery loves company, I confess to having derived some degree of satisfaction on realizing the fact that my tent mate and I were not the only ones making that fatal mistake on that dark and dismal night.

To go into details of our prison life, of the weary days and nights of slow but sure starvation and misery, would require too much space; sufficient to say that the 200 or more men captured on that dark, rainy night from Kilpatrick's command were treated with marked and special rigor by the prison authorities at Richmond, keeping us exclusively by ourselves on the fourth floor of the Pemberton Warehouse. On reaching our prison, a thorough search of our persons and a systematic robbery of our money, jewels and valuables of whatsoever description found on each individual, was inaugurated, even the taking of the cherished pictures of friends at home were not exempted. When I saw the photo of the girl I had left behind me transferred from the pocket nearest my heart into Rebel hands, I offered a mild resistance and was answered with the chivalrous and complimentary remark, "You d—d Yankee, you have been in some house and stole that." After I became better acquainted with these strutting dignitaries and their ways I wondered that the searcher did not knock me down with the butt of his pistol or loaded whip instead of paying me the compliment he did.

After spending three weeks in Pemberton, the Rebel authorities concluded that it would not be an entirely safe policy to "Hang those 200 Yanks" that General Hampton apprehended, "as the Richmond papers advised," so we were conveyed to Belle Isle and permitted to share the bed of Mother Earth with leaky tents and raw corn meal in very limited quantities, as had fared the several thousands of unfortunate Union prisoners who had spent the winter there before us. In May we were transferred to and confined, for reasons unknown to us, in the notorious "Libby" prison. In July I parted company with my unfortunate and cherished Comrade Daily, I being sent to the Columbian Hospital, suffering from scurvey and other troubles, and he to Andersonville, where his bones lie bleaching, dying there three weeks after we parted company.

In the loss of Corporal Daily, Co. "E" and the 7th Michigan Cavalry lost one of its truest, best and bravest soldiers.

On the 11th day of August, "happy day," I was paroled

with many sick and wounded and conveyed by boat to Camp Parole, Annapolis, Md. In December I rejoined the Regiment at its winter quarters near Winchester, Va., fully determined never again, under any circumstances, to be taken prisoner. From there I followed the fortunes of the Regiment to its final muster out of service, including the final "round up" at Appomattox, and across the plains to the Rockies and back to Fort Leavenworth, where I received my final discharge.

In conclusion, I would say that I have made Comrade C. Y. McClain due and satisfactory apologies for having lost his "Spencer."

1864.   1900.

Geo. W. Watson,
Co. "E."
Lansing, Mich.

Born at Red Creek, Wayne County, N. Y., September 6th, 1844; enlisted at Jackson, Jackson County, Mich., September 9th, 1864, as Private in Co. "E," 7th Michigan Cavalry; mustered out at Fort Leavenworth, Kansas, July 17th, 1865, and honorably discharged.

UNDER COMMAND OF GEN. SHERIDAN.
By Geo. W. Watson.

My first acquaintance with General Sheridan was at the battle of Cedar Creek, October 19th, 1864. About 3 p. m. I found myself on the right of the skirmish line across the road from a brick house. I saw a horseman coming across the fields on a black horse covered with foam. He leaped the stone fence in front of the house. There was not a Staff Officer in sight, and as there were a number of stragglers in the road and about the house, Sheridan said: "Boys, come back and we will give them h—l," and he quickly made his word good.

I was detailed for picket one day in January, 1865, on the out-posts. It was a very cold night, and after I had been relieved, I turned in by the fire and, being a novice at the business, pulled off my boots and went to sleep. Soon there was a gun fired on the picket line and we had orders to turn out and mount. The result was I found my boots frozen so hard that I could not get them on, so I mounted with boots in one hand and reins in the other. As it was a false alarm we were soon back to camp and I thawed those boots out, and I assure you I was never caught that way again.

Co F

GRAND ARMY OF THE REPUBLIC
1861 · VETERAN · 1866

1862.   1901.

STEPHEN B. MANN,

Captain Co. "F,"

Glenwood, Fla.

Born in the County of Tioga, Penn., March 23rd, 1832; enlisted at Detroit, Mich., August 14th, 1862, as First Lieutenant in Co. "G," 5th Michigan Cavalry; transferred and promoted to Captain of Co. "F," 7th Michigan Cavalry, October 15th, 1862; discharged at Washington, D. C., July 8th, 1863, without resignation by order of Board of Surgeons by special order for physical disability and honorably discharged.

REMINISCENCES.
By Stephen B. Mann.

My experience with the old 7th was short and of no importance to add to its history. The Regiment, as you know, was sent from Grand Rapids to Washington in the dead of winter. We were a lot of raw recruits without drill or discipline, but made up of the very stuff that afterwards proved to be the best. Our first business on going into camp at Washington was to drill our men as best we could. The weather was bad, and the mud on our drill-ground was knee deep or more with snow and slush, but before we had become at all proficient we were ordered to march to actual duty. No arms were issued to the men except revolvers. We started from our camp at 9 o'clock at night over the "Long Bridge," marched all night and till noon or after the next day, when we halted in an open field, as we supposed, to wait for our baggage wagons to come up. Soon a heavy rain set in with relentless fury, and kept it up till near night, when it turned to snow, which was ten inches deep in the morning and frozen hard, while we had no fire or shelter of any kind. Many of our horses died and one or two men also, for my part I soon came down with pneumonia and was sent to hospital.

After leaving the hospital I was of little use as a soldier and the doctor ordered me to Washington to report to headquarters, ordering an ambulance to take me there. Distasteful as this was, there seemed no other way. I reported as soon as I could to the Surgeon's office for treatment, but was told it was useless as I had consumption and would die soon, etc. I was advised at headquarters to resign and go home. To this I strongly demurred, fully believing I would recover and be able to take my place with the boys. I was then told that by a special order I might be discharged on Surgeon's certificate, the same as a private soldier, which discharge would be more honorable than to resign. I was again assured that I could not live very long, and it was my duty to my country and to myself to get out of the way of some stronger man to take my place in the field. This sort of argument prevailed and I accepted the discharge.

So now, Comrades, you see I can add no great glory to the valiant old 7th by any daring deed of mine. I went in with as high hopes as any of those who covered themselves all over with glory, but was cut off too early to show whether there was the real qualities of a soldier in me or not. However, I honor the old 7th and am proud to have my name on her roll.

May the choicest of earth's blessings be for you all, and may you attend many more Reunions, with many honors to crown the silvered locks that will gather at each Reunion.

1864   1901

Dr. Asa B. Isham,

First Lieutenant Co. "F."

849 Oak St., Walnut Hills, Cincinnati, Ohio.

Born July 12th, 1844, at Jackson C. H., Jackson County, Ohio; enlisted at Detroit, Mich., November 18th, 1862, as Private of Co. "I," 7th Michigan Cavalry; promoted to Sergeant and Regimental Clerk and Marker; severely wounded in action near Warrentown Junction, Va., May 14th, 1863; First Lieutenant March 22nd, 1864; slightly wounded below the knee and taken prisoner in action at Yellow Tavern, Va., May 11th, 1864; confined in Libby Prison, at Macon and Savannah, Georgia, Charleston and Columbia, S. C.; paroled for exchange December 10th, 1864, at Charleston, S. C., at which place had been under fire of our batteries on Morris Island for six weeks in September and October; exchanged December 11th, 1864; honorably discharged for disability arising from wounds received in action April 14th, 1865.

YELLOW TAVERN.
MAJOR HENRY W. GRANGER—GEN. J. E. B. STUART.
By Asa B. Isham.

Yellow Tavern was, undoubtedly, the greatest Cavalry contest of the War, considering the forces engaged and the results achieved for the Union arms. My comrades will recall that the order of the Regiment for that 11th day of May, 1864, was "left in front by inversion," which brought Co. "F" to the front, and, myself, as ranking officer, in command of the first squadron composed of Cos. "F" and "G." As we were drawn up in line, mounted, behind the woods, in which were the 5th and 6th Michigan Regiments, dismounted, my end of the line overlapped the angle of the woods. I sat my horse facing the Rebel battery of six guns upon the hill, about three-quarters of a mile away, and every flash of its guns was not only visible but appealed to my imagination in the most unquestionable way that the undesirable contents were traveling in a straight line toward my anatomy. In fact a small piece of shell did strike me upon the outer side of the left leg below the knee. About the time that I was beginning to think that it was in the highest degree requisite that the relations of myself and the battery should be changed in some manner, my attention was diverted by what appeared to be a tornado sweeping in the rear. It was the 1st Michigan Cavalry, in column of squadrons, moving at the trot. It wheeled upon my flank as a pivot with beautiful precision, and came to a halt a little in advance of me, squarely in front and in full view of the Rebel guns. It had, just previous to starting upon the campaign, returned from veteran furlough with its ranks recruited to one thousand men. In squadron front it covered over two hundred and fifty feet by one hundred and twenty in depth, and it formed a weight of six hundred tons that was about to be hurled across the fields and ravines upon that battery and its supports. It was a magnificent engine of warfare, and I somehow began to feel a contempt for the Rebel cannon, which had inspired me with profound solicitude but a few minutes before. I sat straight up in my saddle and cheered in admiration of the 1st Michigan Cavalry, and in derision of the artillery, although the latter was now pelting away more lustily than ever. This splendid body of horsemen was halted but for a moment, when General Custer reined in at the head of it with an order to 'charge," and away it went toward the guns. It was swallowed up in dust and smoke, a volume of exulting shouts smote the air, the earth shook and it was evident that a besom of destruction was sweeping over the face of nature. Five fences and a bridge made six breaks in the formation, but as many times was the column reformed, and the height was carried as a finish, to the great discomfiture of the Confederates. It was as fine a Regiment of Cavalry as was ever hurled against a foe, most gallantly did it push the charge, and, as we followed it "by fours" to the hill from which the Rebels had been dislodged, my horse felt as though he was an elephant under me and my head was among the clouds; because I had a feeling that I was riding along with heroes, and I did not give a —— picayune where we might pull up.

When Major Granger gave the order to charge, and dashed down the declivity leading to the Telegraph road, I repeated the order to the command, stuck the spurs into my steed and followed him. After we had passed over the barricade in the road and struck the Rebel column of "fours," we were riding nearly neck and neck. Even at that time some of the troopers from behind had forged ahead of us. The Major was firing with his revolver over the neck of my horse at a group of Confederates about a battle flag in the woods, a little to the left of our line of charge. As I have already narrated, in our Regimental History, General J. E. B. Stuart was among that group of horsemen and the banner displayed was his Corps ensign. On account of the dust and smoke of battle I did not notice a rise of the ground to our left and remarked to the Major that he was firing high. Major Granger, however, undoubtedly appreciated the "lay" of the ground, and knew at whom he was firing, as he had, when a Lieutenant of the New York Lincoln Cavalry, met General Stuart under a flag of true. From the earnestness with which the Major was directing his fire at the horsemen about the battle flag, instead of immediately in his front, particularly as he was upon my right and had to direct his aim over my horse, I am pursuaded that he was shooting at General Stuart with a full knowledge of whom he was firing upon, and that it was a pistol shot from his revolver that ended the life of the Confederate Cavalry chief. He could not have been shot by one of the 1st Michigan Cavalry, for that Regiment was not within pistol or even carbine range of him at the time he fell.

My observation of the Major occupied but an instant of time. My horse leaped an obstruction, perhaps a horse that had gone down before him—or it may have been at this time that he was struck by a ball in the shoulder—and, I saw no more of Major Granger. Just at this time I made a thrust with the point of my saber at the neck of a burly Confederate, but whether or not any damage was inflicted upon him I do not know, as he was blotted from view by dust and smoke, and the scene was changed, when once more vision was unclouded. A young trooper of Co. "C," whose name is lost beyond recall in the lapse of years, who had somehow worked to the front from near the rear of the column, always insisted that I had saved his life by unhorsing a big rebel who was about to cut him down. Of this, however, I know nothing. Co. "C." always had a reputation for romancing, and I have always suspected this as a fairy tale by one of the Company's most impressionable boys. Whether or not the now unknown "C" trooper was dealing in fiction, it may be said to his credit that in the Spring of 1865, near Grafton, West Virgina, he quelled a mutiny among a lot of paroled prisoners in transit from Annapolis,

Md., to St. Louis, Mo., and prevented an assault upon four officers disabled by wounds, who had them in charge without a guard, upon the ground that I had saved his life in action with the enemy, and that a sentiment of common gratitude demanded that the authority of such an officer should be respected.

When, near the end of the battle, Captains Loomis and Fisher pushed their companies up the Telegraph road, they found the body of Major Granger about fifty yards beyond the barricade and nearly opposite the position occupied by General Stuart and his staff. He had been struck by three balls in different parts, any one of which was necessarily mortal, so that his death must have been instantaneous. General Stuart's wound was not immediately fatal. He was removed from the field and lived until the next day. Thus passed away two brave men in the very prime of life.

1899.

GEORGE FERRIS,
Lieutenant Co. "F."
Dead.

Born at Eaton Rapids, Mich., January 31st, 1840; enlisted at Eaton Rapids, Mich., September 9th, 1862, as private in Co. "D," 7th Michigan Cavalry; promoted to Second Lieutenant February 28th, 1864, and to First Lieutenant May 24th, 1865, and transferred to First Michigan Veteran Cavalry November 17th, 1865; mustered out at Salt Lake City, Utah, March 10th, 1866, and honorably discharged. Was killed near Rawlins, Wyoming, at Ferris Haggarty Mine, August 20th, 1900, by his horses becoming frightened and dashing down a steep pitch, throwing him out.

1898.

HARMON SMITH,
Lieutenant Co. "F."
Orleans, Ionia Co., Mich.

Born March 6th, 1833, at Ballstown, Seneca County, N. Y.; enlisted at Prairieville, Barry County, Mich., December 27th, 1862, as Sergeant in Co. "F," 7th Michigan Cavalry; was promoted to Second Lieutenant December 12th, 1865; was wounded at Smithfield, Va., August 27th, 1864, in right foot while in action; was mustered out December 15th, 1865, at Leavenworth, Kan., and was honorably discharged at Jackson, Mich., December 25th, 1865.

CO. "F" AT THE BATTLE OF TREVILIAN'S STATION.
By Harmon Smith.

In the eventful history of our magnificent Regiment it is no easy task to specify events, but it seems appropriate to give some attention to the events of June 11th and 12th at Trevilian's Station.

On the morning of the 11th I was in command of Co. "F" as Ranking Officer, and had nineteen men at roll-call. Before we had tasted our coffee we were charged by Confederate Cavalry from the direction of Louisa Court House. As I remember, it was my Company who drove back this charge, and following up the Rebels I almost forgot the rear of my own command, and upon looking about I saw my whole force in rapid motion going away from us and in the direction of the Station, my horse with the lot. By an almost superhuman effort I gained the column and my horse; we were soon at the Station with fighting here at the front, in the rear, at the right and at the left.

It was my fortune to be near Gen. Custer, and of course in the middle of the fray. One officer was so muddled that he asked Custer if it would not be best to move certain things for safety to the rear. The General said, "Yes, by all means," and then added, "Where in hell is the rear?" By this time the Brigade was scattered in many directions, but as the battle progressed and the artillery being with Custer, the different parts gradually gathered at the Station. We repelled five heavy charges made to capture one big gun. In one of these charges a large part of the Rebel Cavalry got one of our pieces in their control and tried to disable it, but a force of seventy-five to one hundred of our boys made a saber charge, one of the sharpest hand-to-hand contests I ever witnessed, and recaptured it. The Commander of the Battery stood gallantly by his gun. One of the Johnnies stunned him by a saber stroke. It was my privilege to take after this chap, a Johnnie took after me, Lieutenant Lyon after the Johnnie, another Johnnie after Lyon, and another Yankee after him. This all happened in a moment's time, but we held the gun, and as the Rebels got out the Artillery boys sallied into them, letting the Johnnies have three shots, Boom,

Bang, Bang. As the smoke cleared away there were five of our men and fifteen Johnnies lying dead. I never knew as to what became of all in the race farther than the fellow ahead of me went down, and Lyon said the one after me followed suit. He was no good with the saber, as he gave me five blows on the back, any of which with a well directed point would have run me through.

It was in one of these charges where Custer's Color-bearer was killed, and the General stripped the colors from the staff and thrust them in his bosom and over his shoulder.

About noon the Rebels seemed to have got enough and drew off to better their position, and we discovered that we had been fighting the whole Rebel Army of the Shenandoah. In the afternoon they were after us again, and as the fray opened the N. Y. Brigade broke through the line and came to our relief, for we had been surrounded from the first. We were now full masters of the field and we tore up several miles of railroad.

I did not see much of the next day's doings until towards night when we tried to carry the railroad on the right, and I always thought this was done to enable us to let the Rebels go.

I saw the noble Lieutenant Nichols of "H" go down in the timber at my side with many others, and as our men were falling back I went with them and as soon as I found the Regiment I got my place in line and at roll-call I had five and only five of my nineteen men, the rest—some of them with the "Great Majority," some prisoners, etc. This was the lowest point in numbers Co. "F" ever reached.

This is substantially as I remember the Battle of Trevilian's Station. General Custer lost his headquarters, I believe, but on the 11th we certainly whipped the whole Rebel Army of the Shenandoah.

1865.   1897.

CHAS. P. WHITE,

Sergeant Co. "F."

Litchfield, Mich.

Born at Scipio, Hillsdale County, Mich., August 28th, 1838; enlisted at Litchfield, Hillsdale County, Mich., November 20th, 1862, as Private in Co. "F," 7th Michigan Cavalry; promoted to Corporal January 1st, 1863, and to Sergeant May 1st, 1865; my first absence from the Regiment was when taken prisoner July 6th, 1863, between Funkstown and Hagerstown, Md., while on detached duty with Lieutenant Newman picking up horses to mount the dismounted men; was taken to Stanton, thence to Belle Isle, Va., reaching there July 24th, remained there until February 11th, 1864; then taken to Libby Prison, remaining there only three days when I was sent with others to Andersonville, Ga., being there until September 8th, when I was taken to Savannah, Ga., and was there until October 16th; from Savannah was taken to Camp Lawton or Millen Stockade and was paroled from there November 23rd, 1864, and sent to Annapolis, making in all five hundred and five consecutive days in prison. "I need not try to tell what I endured and suffered in those prisons, McIlroy tells it too plainly." On arriving at Annapolis I got a furlough for fifty days and came home to Michigan; was exchanged, and reported at Dismounted Camp, Pleasant Valley, Md.; was with the dismounted men after Booth in Maryland and then went to Washington, joining the Regiment the day before the Grand Review; went with the Regiment to Fort Leavenworth and then on the Western campaign to the summit of the Rockies and back to Fort Collins; from there was with a detachment of twenty-five under command of Lieutenant J. Q. A. Sessions to Denver, Colo., and over the Smoky Hill Route to Fort Leavenworth, Kansas, where I was mustered out November 25th, 1865, and honorably discharged.

1899.

Clark H. Beardslee,

Co. "F."

Marcellus, Mich.

Born December 17th, 1845, at Marshall, Calhoun County, Mich.; enlisted at Sheridan, Calhoun County, Mich., December 30th, 1862, as Private in Co. "F," 7th Michigan Cavalry; was wounded at Falling Waters July 14th, 1863, in right thigh, and at Coal Harbor May 30th, 1864, in right leg below the knee; was taken prisoner June 11, 1864, at Trevilian's Station, Va., and was in Libby, Andersonville, Millen, and Savannah Prisons; was mustered out at Fort Leavenworth, Kan., November 21st, 1865, and honorably discharged.

1889.

Joseph Doherty,

Co. "F."

208 Fischer Ave., Detroit, Mich.

Born at Bristol, England, September 19th, 1843; enlisted at Detroit, Wayne County, Mich., January 10th, 1863, as Private in Co. "F," 7th Michigan Cavalry; wounded September, 1863, at Rapidan, by gun shot wounds in right forearm and left shoulder; taken prisoner September 17th, 1863, and taken to Pemberton, Va.; Libby, Va.; Belle Isle, Va.; Andersonville, Ga.; Camp Lawton, Ga.; Salisbury, N. C.; was recaptured by the 11th Michigan Cavalry at Salisbury, N. C., April, 1865; mustered out at Harper Hospital, Detroit, Mich., September 8th, 1865, and honorably discharged.

1899.

NATHAN H. SPACE,

Co. "F."

Grand Ledge, Eaton Co., Mich.

Born April 8th, 1843, at Upper Sandusky, Ohio; enlisted February, 1864, in Co. "F," 7th Michigan Cavalry; captured June 11th, 1864, at Trevilian's Station, Va., conducted to Libby Prison and from there to Andersonville, from which prison he and Comrade N. R. Billings, of Co. "F," escaped September 15th; was recaptured September 21st and immediately returned to Andersonville, where he was met by the black-hearted Wirz, who cursed him and ordered him put into stocks for eight hours without food or drink. In November was transferred to the Savannah Prison and from there paroled and exchanged and mustered out at Fort Leavensworth, Kas., February 2d, 1866, and honorably discharged.

ONE EXPERIENCE.
By N. H. Space.

In May, 1864, our Regiment was on the picket line at Coal Harbor, Va.; Comrades McComb, Dudley and myself were placed in advance of the regular line with strict orders to fire if we heard a noise in front. We soon discovered there was a wounded soldier about ten rods from us in our front, who kept continually groaning and calling for water. As day began to break I decided I would venture over and give him a drink and place him more comfortable and where he could be cared for. I found on reaching him that he was a Confederate. He drank freely from my canteen, and just as he finished I heard these words from him: "Yank, over here." Looking up I saw a Confederate with gun in hand ready to fire. Knowing my carbine was both loaded and cocked I resolved to fire; both guns were discharged at the same time; where my bullet went I never knew, but the Confederate's bullet took a little skin off my cheek, just enough to start the blood. I ran back to our lines and was followed by a volley from the Rebs, which volley killed Comrade McComb.

1864. 1901.

WILLIAM F. KENFIELD,

Co. "F."

Woonsocket, Sanborn Co., S. D.

Born at Hastings, Barry County, Mich., June 30th, 1846; enlisted at Grand Rapids, Kent County, Mich., February 29th, 1864, as Private in Co. "F," 7th Michigan Cavalry; mustered out at Fort Leavenworth, Kansas, November 21st, 1865, and honorably discharged.

TREVILIAN'S STATION.

By William F. Kenfield.

The Battle of Trevilian's Station, fought June 11th and 12th, 1864, has been generally conceded by the men of the Michigan Cavalry Brigade, who were in that fight to have been as desperate as any, if not the most desperate, of the war, lasting two full days.

The Brigade bivouaced the night of June 10th about five miles from the Station that has become historical, and near to the North Anna River.

The next day dawned warm and clear. Our Regiment was the first to be attacked by the Confederates, led by General Wade Hampton, and with scarcely any warning. I was preparing a sumptuous (?) breakfast, composed of bacon and flapjacks, when the attack was made, but in my haste to get to a safer place with my horse and accoutrements I did not taste it. The Brigade was under the command of General Custer, the idol of his troopers and the terror of his foes. We were soon surrounded and fighting became fast and furious. I was cut off from my Regiment in a mix up about eleven a. m. and became attached to a party numbering about fifty and composed mostly of the 5th and 7th Michigan Cavalry boys. We were a badly demoralized lot. Belden, our Regimental saddler, and I think a Captain of the 1st Michigan Cavalry, lagged behind at a plantation house and were picked up in our very sight. Finally, we halted in a piece of woods and held a sort of council of war, with the result that I was selected to take command. Being promised implicit obedience, I consented, though not without reluctance, owing to my youth and short service.

I selected four men to act as flankers and then moved in an easterly direction, avoiding all traveled roads. We later captured two of Fitzhugh Lee's troopers who were making a sneak to their homes near by. All went well until about dusk when soon after emerging from the cover of the woods and while passing through a narrow defile, a band of guerillas attacked us without the slightest warning. Lewis Adams, of Co. "L," 5th Michigan Cavalry, and myself only escaped. We had fine mounts and were fully determined not to surrender unless compelled to, so putting spurs to our horses we led the guerillas a merry chase, and though at no time did any of them get within twenty yards of us, even at that distance they were uncomfortably close and determined to wing us if possible and howling like a lot of demons. Fearing they might ride us down and not relishing their target practice, we jumped from our horses and plunged into a thicket. Darkness was closing in and we felt comparatively safe for the time being. Tired, hungry, thirsty and much disheartened, we sank down at last under a spreading oak and, back to back, with the rain falling on us we soon forgot all our troubles. Once only were we awakened during the night and that by the sound of footsteps close by; they soon died away and we were again oblivious of our desperate straits. Adams wakened me early the next morning, my clothes were wet and steaming, and the birds were singing sweetly in the boughs overhead. It was some moments before I realized my sad plight. I learned several years later from one of the party, who lost his legs by scurvy in Andersonville Prison, that nine of the boys fell with the guerillas' first fire and that all save Adams and myself were taken prisoners. He also said that the guerillas were very angry because of Adams and my escape, and that we undoubtedly would have been killed if taken for refusing to surrender when the rest did.

There were thrilling incidents in store for us that day, a detailed recital of which would fill a small book. Finally, about five o'clock p. m. we heard for the first time after being cut off, the sound of cannon and immediately started on a run in the direction of the firing, scarcely halting for breath, until we reached a negro hut that lay in our course. We found the owner of the place (a freedman) willing to aid us, but he being ignorant as to the position of the contending forces, we sent him ahead to reconnoitre. At last we crossed our lines near a Field Hospital, which was then being shelled. Here

Adams and I parted. Assistant Surgeon Beach, of the 5th Michigan Cavalry, kindly gave me some hardtack and made a place for me in an army wagon. Our forces retreated under cover of darkness. The jolting I got that night was something fearful, and the curses of the driver when the wagon would strike a pile of rails or other obstruction, were loud and long. I found my Regiment after several days' search and my return was a great surprise to the boys, I having been reported killed. Through the kindness of that brave patriot, Colonel Brewer, who received his death wound during the last charge of our forces at the Battle of Winchester, September 19th, 1864, I was furnished a horse and fell into my accustomed place, thankful that I was alive. Shortly after our command rejoined Grant's Army I was stricken with fever and saw nothing of my Regiment until the following December. I was appointed Regimental Mail Carrier soon after my return to the Regiment and served in that capacity until after the close of the war.

Adams survived many years, dying near Kalamazoo, Mich., in 1901.

A great majority of the grand old Brigade whose exploits have become a part of the history of the great Civil War, and whose deeds are preserved in song and story, in bronze and marble, have answered their final roll call. A goodly remnant, however, yet linger "in the shadows." May their declining years be made easy and their end be peaceful.

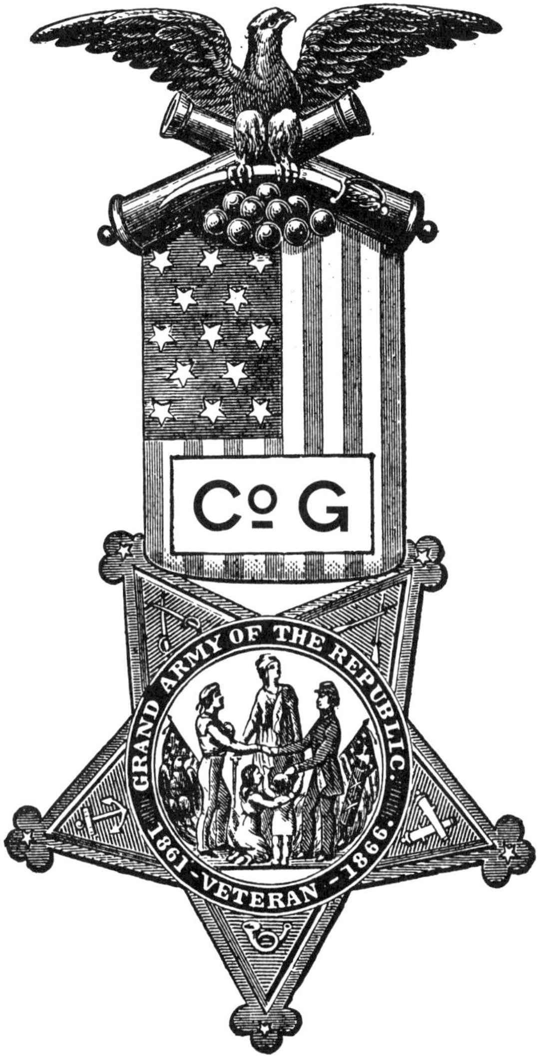
Co G
GRAND ARMY OF THE REPUBLIC
1861 - VETERAN - 1866.

1864

1901

GEORGE W. HILL,
Lieutenant Co. "G."
Dead.

Born at Ypsilanti, Mich., April 21st, 1839; enlisted at Detroit, Mich., August 16th, 1862, in 5th Michigan Cavalry; transferred to 7th Michigan Cavalry December 3rd, 1862; mustered as Second Lieutenant of Co. "C" January 24th, 1863, made First Lieutenant of Co. "G" May 24th, 1865; taken prisoner in action at Yellow Tavern, Va., May 11th, 1864, exchanged March 1st, 1865; transferred to 1st Michigan Veteran Cavalry November 17th, 1865; mustered out at Salt Lake City, Utah, March 10th, 1866, and honorably discharged. Died the morning of September 3rd, 1901.

Comrade Hill was found dead in his home, 76 Piquette avenue, by his family, supposing to have died between 6 and 7 that morning. The cause of his death was attributed to apoplexy. His pallbearers were four members of the 7th Michigan Cavalry and two comrades from Detroit G. A. R. Post, which Post had charge of the funeral. He was buried at Ypsilanti, Mich., his boyhood home.

1902.

BUTLER S. TUBBS,

Lieutenant Co. "G."

Rose, Oakland Co., Mich.

Born May 28th, 1833, at Southport, Chenango County, N. Y.; enlisted at Fenton, Genesee County, Mich., August 24th, 1862, as Corporal of Co. "I," 6th Michigan Cavalry; transferred and promoted to Sergeant October 15th, 1862, of Co. "G," 7th Michigan Cavalry; promoted to Second Lieutenant March 24th, 1865, and promoted to First Lieutenant May 26th, 1865, not mustered; transferred to 1st Michigan Veteran Cavalry November 17th, 1865; mustered out at Salt Lake City, Utah Ter., March 10th, 1866, and honorably discharged.

1863.   1901.

WILLIAM C. BARDEN,

Com. Sergeant Co. "G."

465 Upton Ave., Battle Creek, Mich.

Born at Leslie, Ingham County, Mich., September 7th, 1842; enlisted at Jackson, Jackson County, Mich., December 24th, 1862, as Private in Co. "G," 7th Michigan Cavalry; was promoted to Corporal March 1st, 1863, 3rd Duty Sergeant September 1st, 1864, Commissary Sergeant April 1st, 1865; taken prisoner on the Kilpatrick Raid to Richmond the spring of 1864, but made my escape the same night; mustered out at Omaha, Neb., December 28, 1865, and honorably discharged.

I had just commenced my winter term of school when the idea struck me to enlist. My seatmate and chum was Martin R. Delamater. One day I said, "Mart, let us enlist," he asked. "Do you mean it?" I said, "Yes," and we then and there shook hands under the old school desk, threw our books across the school-room against the blackboard just as recess was ordered, and rushed out, nor did we return again until noon for our books.

In the meantime we had informed our parents that we were going to enlist and they gave us to understand that they would not give their consent, therefore we had to make a flank movement, so we arranged to meet at our barn at midnight and if he got there first to wait for me and if I got there first I would wait for him. We did not trust ourselves to sleep that night, and just as the old clock struck twelve, and I could hear my father snoring; I quietly slipped into my clothes and taking my boots in my hands softly raised the window and crawled out on a low shed and silently dropped to the ground just in time to see Mart coming through the gate. Previously supplying ourselves with a few biscuits and doughnuts, we started for Jackson, seventeen miles away, to enlist. After about a six-mile walk we reached Grand River to find that the low lands had overflowed for a half mile wide and were frozen over with about a quarter of an inch of ice and the water from a foot to two feet deep. Pulling off our boots and stockings we waded through, breaking the ice at every step until we reached the opposite shore, then pulling on our boots and stockings we struck out for Jackson, reaching there at daylight on the morning of December 24th.

We strolled about town until 10 a. m., when we met Lewis Carson, in uniform, and looking for recruits. He hastily conducted us to a Recruiting Office and the examining board being in session we quickly passed inspection and enlisted. Christmas morning, 1862, we were on our way with other recruits for

Grand Rapids to join our Regiment. Poor Mart never came home, being mortally wounded at the Battle of the Wilderness and died in hospital.

During my three years service I never reported to sick call but once, and then threw the medicine away before reaching my tent. Never absent from my Company except on detail or detached service. Had three horses killed under me while in the saddle and participated in eighty-four engagements according to my diary kept of every day from enlistment to discharge.

ATTACKED BY A WOMAN.
By William C. Barden.

While on our raid down the Shenandoah Valley in 1864, burning barns, driving off the stock, etc., two of my companions and myself went to a house some distance from the marching column. One stood picket, the other held my horse, while I investigated the house. Entering with revolver in hand and seeing there was no one but a tall, lean, peaked-nosed woman with eyes like a hawk, I proceeded to investigate. Going down cellar I discovered some apples the size of small hen's eggs and gathering up what I could in my arms started up the dark and narrow stairs to put them in my feed bag, but just as I reached the top steps and was stooping to go through the low door she met me with a heavy iron poker in both hands and with a vengeance whacking me over the left side of my cranium and over my left eye, the blood flowing freely, the apples all dropping back to the bottom of the cellar near where I found them. She made a second pass at me, but I guarded it off and made a spring for her, and as she turned I grabbed her around the waist and arms, her back to me, and the way we sasheed around that room was not slow, she a head taller than myself and kicking back like a mule and spitting over her shoulder into my face; that, with the blood clotting over one eye, was not pleasant. In the meantime Wetherby, who was holding my horse, was laughing at the fun and proceeded to gather up the apples that I had dropped. I then released and gave my lady companion a push from me, kissed my hand to her in a good-bye and sprang into my saddle in time to catch the rear guard as it was passing by. I hastened on and overtook my Company, but it was two long hours before I could find water to wash up. With the air full of smoke and dust and my face covered with blood, etc., I was a sight to behold, and when the boys of the Company found out the scrape I had been in they gave me a big laugh.

1898.

WILLIAM H. HIBBARD,
Sergeant Co. "G."

361 Cass Ave., Detroit, Mich.

Born at Pittsford, Monroe County, N. Y., September 15th, 1844; enlisted at Ypsilanti, Mich., November 15th, 1862, as Private in Co. "G," 7th Michigan Cavalry; promoted to Sergeant October 31st, 1863; mustered out at Fort Leavenworth, Kan., December 15, 1865, and honorably discharged.

MY ADVANCE AND RETREAT FROM AN ISLAND.

By Sergeant William H. Hibbard.

While doing picket duty on the Rappahannock, opposite Fredericksburg, I was Sergeant in charge of a small post with a detachment consisting of a Corporal and nine men. We were camped in the yard of a house in front of a large peach orchard above Falmouth and overlooking the river, our little squad keeping out three picket posts night and day.

A short distance up the river from our post was an island, and on the island a farm and nice buildings. The widest channel of the river was on the Falmouth side, the channel on the Fredericksburg side was much narrower but deeper. One morning the Corporal and I stood looking from the high bank down onto the island, and being both young and, I presume, foolish, I proposed that we go over to the island and see what we could find. He agreed, and going down the bank we started to cross on the rocks, hoping to get over without wetting our feet, but when some distance from the shore we found the rocks too far apart to jump, so going back we got a long pole, and by laying this across on the rocks at the widest places we succeeded in reaching the island. Taking our poles with us we approached the house from the rear, where a high, tight board fence enclosed it and the yard, shutting out any view from the outside. As we reached it we stepped up to the fence together, took hold of the top, and pulling ourselves up, looked over. There we saw eight Rebel Cavalrymen with their horses in the yard, enjoying the hospitality of the owner of the house. The recognition was mutual, and two soldiers wearing blue coats had important business toward camp, and eight boys in Gray helped them to make good time by a few shots from their revolvers. I think I never made better time than on that run to the river, and every shot the Johnnies fired helped me to let out another link. We both reached the river safely and needed no pole to cross on, neither did we miss a rock nor wet our feet. Close to the bank on the other side of the river was a large rock, behind which we dropped to shelter us from the bullets which were coming fast and thick, and were no sooner behind the rock than one of the Johnnies called out, "Say, Yank, we won't shoot any more," so we got up and sat on the rock, and they had a good laugh at us. One of them said, "Yanks, you'uns ought to have seen how you'uns looked while running," and I answered him, "You ought to have known how we felt."

Compiler wonders what Corporal Barden was doing about that time.

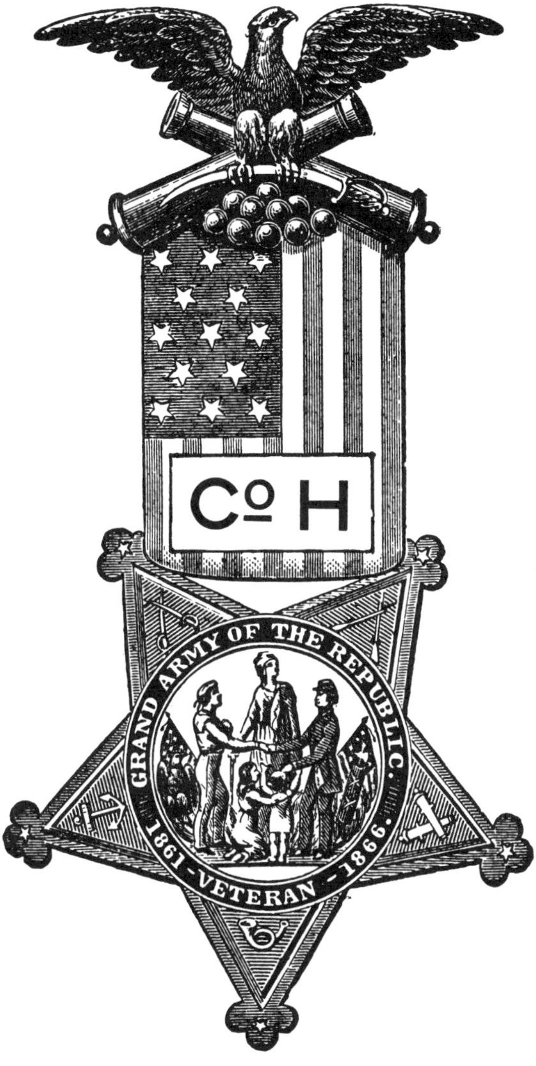
Co H
GRAND ARMY OF THE REPUBLIC.
1861 - VETERAN - 1866.

1864.

Frank B. Clark,

Lieutenant Co. "H."

Dead.

Born near Port Stanley, Ont., October 19th, 1845; enlisted at Pontiac, Mich., November 24th, 1862, as Private in Co. "E," 7th Michigan Cavalry; promoted to Corporal and then to Sergeant in 1863, then to Sergeant-Major and made Second Lieutenant May 22nd, 1864, promoted to First Lieutenant and Adjutant December 12th, 1865, "not mustered as First Lieutenant;" mustered out at Salt Lake City, Utah Territory, May 10th, 1866, and honorably discharged; killed by accidental discharge of his own revolver in the spring of 1866 enroute to Fort Leavenworth, Kansas, with a detachment of mustered out men. He was a brave, true and faithful soldier, a companionable and lovable friend, and his memory will ever be fresh with those associated with him in war or peace.

1902.

WILLIAM FISHER,

Co. "H."

Richland, Kalamazoo Co., Mich.

Born in Yates County, N. Y., March 14th, 1844; enlisted at Kalamazoo, Kalamazoo County, Mich., December 14th, 1862, as Private in Co. "H," 7th Michigan Cavalry; wounded at Berryville, W. Va., September 4th, 1864, by shell in left foot, same shell killing seven horses; mustered out at Fort Leavenworth, Kansas, December 15th, 1865, and honorably discharged.

AN INCIDENT.

By William Fisher.

At the Battle of Yellow Tavern, Va., May 10th, 1863, I thought "Billy" Kemp and John Brackett, of my Company, had a couple of prisoners. They had gone over the brush fence lining the road toward the enemy and had captured two Rebels, who were strapping big fellows, black-whiskered, and to my eyes were as tall men as I had ever seen. All at once I noticed there was trouble, it looking as though the tables had been turned and instead of prisoners they appeared to be the captors. It looked hard for Billy and John; suddenly my "Spencer" spoke just once and there remained but one Rebel, and he was doing his best to get out of range, which he finally succeeded in doing. Kemp was on our side of the fence in short order, minus prisoners and thankful to be alive. He inquired of me, "Did you fire that shot?"

"Yes," I replied; "I saw you were in trouble with chances against you and did it to save you." Billy replied, "Well, it was well you did, as that shot saved my life."

Poor Comrade Brackett was never seen again after the prisoner escaped, all trace of him being lost from that moment.

1864.   1901.

Arthur Longman,

Co. "H."

617 Oak St., Kalamazoo, Mich.

Born in Yorkshire, England, October 6th, 1845; enlisted at Battle Creek, Calhoun County, Mich., August 18th, 1864, as Private in Co. "H," 7th Michigan Cavalry,; wounded in right leg below the knee by kick of horse while marching at night near Petersburg about March 25th, 1865; mustered out at Fort Leavenworth, Kansas, July 17th, 1865, and honorably discharged.

REMINISCENCE.

By Arthur Longman.

I joined my Regiment on the battlefield of Winchester, September 19th, 1864, just one month from the day I was mustered in. Was with the Regiment on the raid in the Shenandoah Valley from one end to the other in the fall of 1864, taking part in the capture of several of Mosby's Command at Front Royal; witnessed the shooting of three and the hanging of four by order of General Custer in retaliation for the killing of prisoners taken from our Brigade; was in the seven days raid in Loudon County, Va., being one of the scouting party that found the corrall of hogs that the enemy had gathered up for the use of their army. We appropriated them to our own use, driving them back to camp, together with the sheep and cattle we had captured; well do I remember this raid. Took part in the engagements at Luray, Port Republic and Mount Crawford; from Mount Crawford I was sent on detail for horses to Harper's Ferry, so missed the Battle of Cedar Creek, October 19th, 1864, joining the Regiment on the field the night after the battle. Soon after we went into winter quarters near Winchester and settled down to picket duty and raiding. Was with the Regiment on the ten days raid the winter of 1864 and 1865 around Gordonsville, Va. mid ice and snow; the second morning out found myself frozen fast to the ground, owing to my clothes having been wet from fording rivers, especially the Rapidan, having to dodge cakes of ice in the passage. We suffered a good deal with cold on this raid and did not inflict much damage to the enemy for we lacked artillery. Returning to camp we continued to do scouting and picket duty until the latter part of February, when we were ordered to get ready to move.

We moved about the 21st day of February, rounded up and captured the last of General Earley's Command and came very near capturing him. This was the hardest marching done by the Brigade while I was with it; for ten days of the time the mud was knee deep to the horses and out of about forty horses that started on the raid belonging to Co. "H," but two were fit for service when we reached White House Landing. After resting a little there the command moved to near City Point, where we drew a fresh supply of horses and moved to near Petersburg, from there we moved on to Lee's Army, taking part in the Battle of Five Forks, capturing the South Side Railroad, then to the Battle of Sailor's Creek, our last hard fight before the surrender, I personally capturing two prisoners in the charge in the scrub timber to the left of our Infantry. I think our Regiment took twice as many prisoners after leaving City Point as we had men. While I was never wounded by shot or shell, still I have drawn my hand over the side of my head and looked for blood after being burned with a ball.

I was on the line in front of Appomattox when the surrender took place, we then moved back to Petersburg, then a forced march to the support of Sherman, marching back to Washington by way of Richmond to take part in the Grand Review. After the Grand Review we were sent to Fort Leavenworth, Kansas, and I was there discharged from service in July, 1865, and returned home feeling that I had seen my share of war for the time that I had served, as with all the rest I had lost by death three bunk mates.

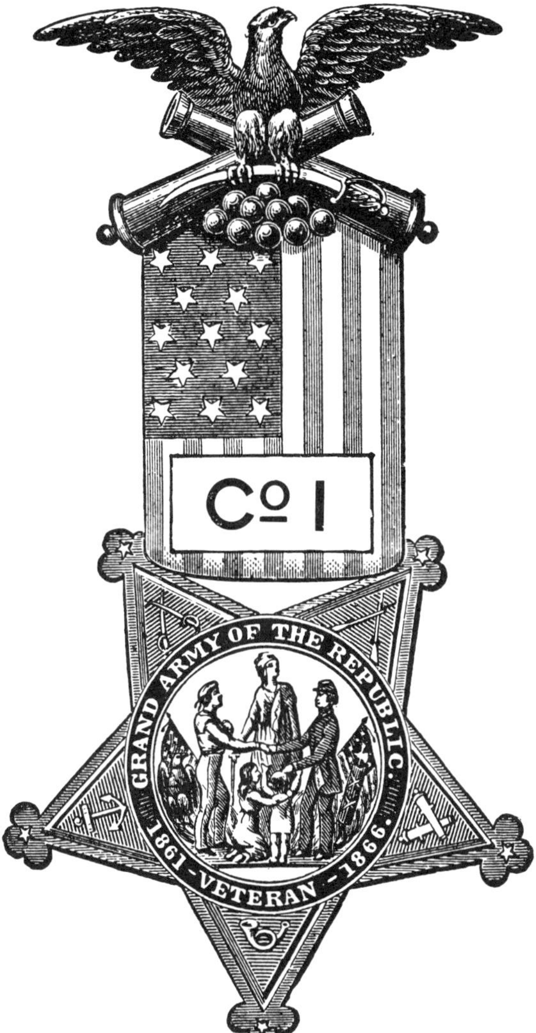
Co I
GRAND ARMY OF THE REPUBLIC
1861 - VETERAN - 1866

1901.

WM. HASTINGS,

Lieutenant Co. "I."

Albion, Mich.

Born May 13th, 1839, at Antrim, Ireland; enlisted at Tecmuseh, Lenawee County, Mich., December 1st, 1862, as Sergeant in Co. "I," 7th Michigan Cavalry; was promoted to First Sergeant in 1864 and to Second Lieutenant May 22d, 1865; was mustered out at Jackson, Mich., December 15th, 1865, and honorably discharged.

COUNTERMANDING GENERAL SHERIDAN'S ORDER IN THE VALLEY.

By Lieutenant Wm. Hastings.

As I have been importuned by our President to give some little reminiscence of my army life, and knowing that I must either do so or be called a "Skulker," a title I always detested, I acquiesce, and here goes the story.

The comrades all remember Sheridan's great raid up the

Shenandoah Valley, at which time he swept almost every living animal that was able to walk out of the valley. Now that the General is dead and the statute of limitation having expired, I will tell in as few words as possible how I countermanded his order.

While passing through Upperville, our Regiment being in the rear, "rather an unusual thing," I happened to see an old lady standing by the front gate crying, while blood flowed from one of her arms. I rode up to her and asked her what was the matter. She told me that in trying to keep her two cows from the soldiers one of them struck her on the arm with his saber. I told her to stop crying and I would get back her cows. After getting a description of them I rode past our own regiment and after a time came up with the Lieutenant in charge of the cattle. I pointed out the two cows and ordered him to turn them back instantly. I also made very strict inquiry for the man who struck the old lady with the saber, but of course he could not be found. The cows I drove back by a circuitous route and left them with their former owner.

Now comes the best part of the story. The old lady had a nice-looking daughter, and she told me that she knew when I started after the cows that I would get them, while the old lady thought that I was just giving her a little sympathy. After getting the cows she invited me to supper, which invitation I declined. The next morning, when we were saddling up, along came the old lady and her daughter and wanted my address. I gave it to them and took theirs in return. The old lady informed me that there was not a man in the world she would rather have her daughter's address than myself, and also told me if ever I was captured by Mosby to have them bring me to Upperville and I should not be hurt.

Comrades, in returning the cows I countermanded General Sheridan's orders, and I hope you will be as lenient with me as he was.

1899

BENJAMIN HULCE,
Co. "I."

Grand Ledge, Mich..

Born at Elmira, Chemung County, N. Y., September 4th, 1829; enlisted September 4th, 1864, as private in Co. I, 7th Michigan Cavalary; mustered out at Detroit, Mich., August 12th, 1865, and honorably discharged.

LEE'S SURRENDER.

By Benjamin Hulce.

I was a recruit, not in the service of my country very long, but ever fresh in my memory is the eventful day of Lee's surrender, April 9th, 1865.

The 7th Michigan Cavalry was called into action before daylight and without breakfast. The enemy was driving us back when a reinforcement of colored troops came to our relief, and glad were we to see them, I can assure you. They were very much excited and were shouting as they leaped over fences, stumps, etc. "We have only a few hours more to fight them, then we will go home and be free." They formed in front of our command when the enemy was obliged to about face and retreat. We followed them to the brink of a long slope where Lee's flag of truce greeted our eyes. Orders came advising us that there would be no more fighting until 4 p. m. We were now ready for breakfast. From the brink we could see Lee and his force in the valley where our officers met them, and beyond on the opposite slope a reinforcement of our men. About 3 p. m. cheers were heard, hats were seen in the air. The Officer of the Day then broke the glad news to us that Lee had surrendered.

1865.   1898.

GEORGE W. BELLINGAR,

Co. "I."

Mount Pleasant, Isabella Co., Mich.

Born at Scipio, Hillsdale County, Mich., December 29th, 1846; enlisted at Mount Pleasant, Isabella County, Mich., February 15th, 1865, as private in Co. "I," 7th Michigan Cavalry; mustered out at Fort Leavenworth, Kansas, December 15th, 1865, and honorably discharged.

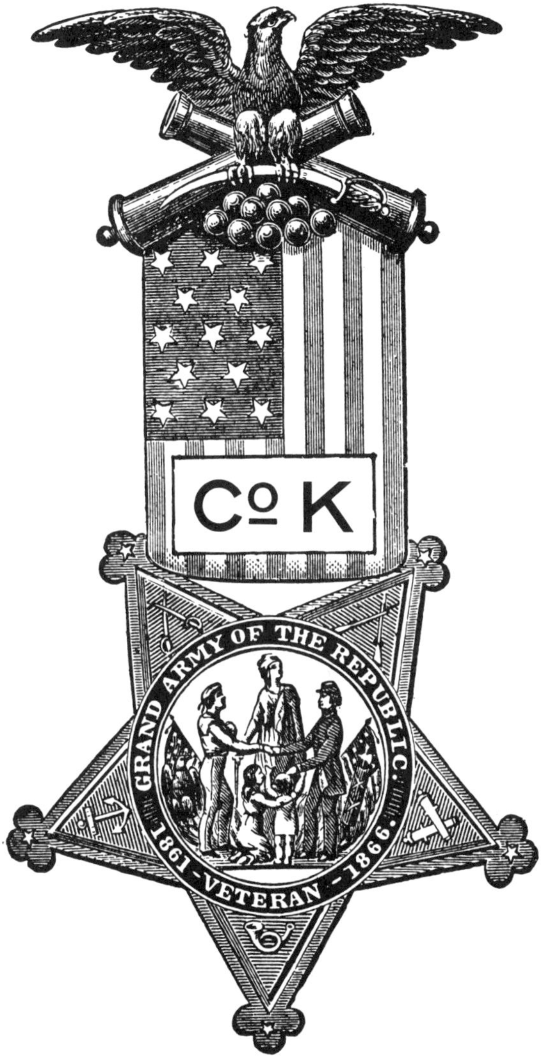
Co K
GRAND ARMY OF THE REPUBLIC.
1861 - VETERAN - 1866.

1864.   1901.

E. W. BARNES,

First Sergeant Co. "K."

Ionia, Mich.

Born at Verona, Oneida County, N. Y., November 4th, 1834; enlisted at Big Prairie, Newaygo County, Mich., November 28th, 1862, as Private in Co. "K," 7th Michigan Cavalry; served through the campaign of 1863, returning to Michigan, December 25th, 1863, with Captain Moore on recruiting service and other duties, acting as Drill Master, Orderly Sergeant, etc. General Custer appointed Wm. Kirkwood and myself Government Detectives and we were sent to Tennessee, Alabama, and other States, our orders at times taking us within the Rebel lines, causing us to run the gauntlet on several occasions. Joined the Regiment just before the Grand Review at Washington, D. C., May, 1865; mustered out at Fort Leavenworth, Kansas, December 15th, 1865, and honorably discharged.

REMINISCENCE.

By E. W. Barnes.

I think Oliver Perry was the first man of the 7th Michigan Cavalry under fire. He was fired on by a member of the 44th Massachusetts, and I suppose they thought they covered themselves with bloodless glory on the event.

In a skirmish at Groveton I was at the right of the skirmish line and having a new horse that had never been under fire, he kept whirling round and made me a splendid target for the Johnnies; how I escaped being hit I never knew. I finally got him started and overtook the command, and when we reached the woods we were dismounted and opened fire on the enemy. J. Downer, my tent mate, and I were together; his gun refused to pull the shell so we sat down on the ground to fix it. While making the repair four Rebel bullets struck between our legs; however, we repaired the gun, joined the advance in the woods and the Rebels were driven back.

In the battle of Brandy Station, I am not positive but I think it was, Downer and myself crossed the railroad in pursuit of two or three Rebels. We kept up the chase with hot firing until we had emptied our revolvers, all the time the Rebels returning our fire; as we came near a piece of woods two more Rebels joined the others, then it was two to one. They ordered us to surrender, but we did not have time; suffice to say we had a sabre fight, which ended in our favor, as only one Johnnie made his escape.

After the Grand Review, as you all know, we were sent to Fort Leavenworth, and from there across the plains to the Rocky Mountains. The morning we started I was put in command of my Company, "K," and was in command of it until sometime in August; Captain Moore being in Michigan and our First Lieutenant under arrest, no Second Lieutenant had been assigned at that time; however, later a Second Lieutenant was assigned and I turned the Company over to him.

I enjoyed the trip and had an easy time as to duties in the Western and Rocky Mountains Campaign. We used to kill antelope, which we cooked in many styles. One day while hunting antelope with Lieutenant Ingersoll and two others, we had a skirmish with a Cinnamon bear, which we did not enjoy or relish at all. Lieutenant Ingersoll said it was the closest call and most fearful moment he ever experienced, as the old Cinnamon fell dead about two feet from him.

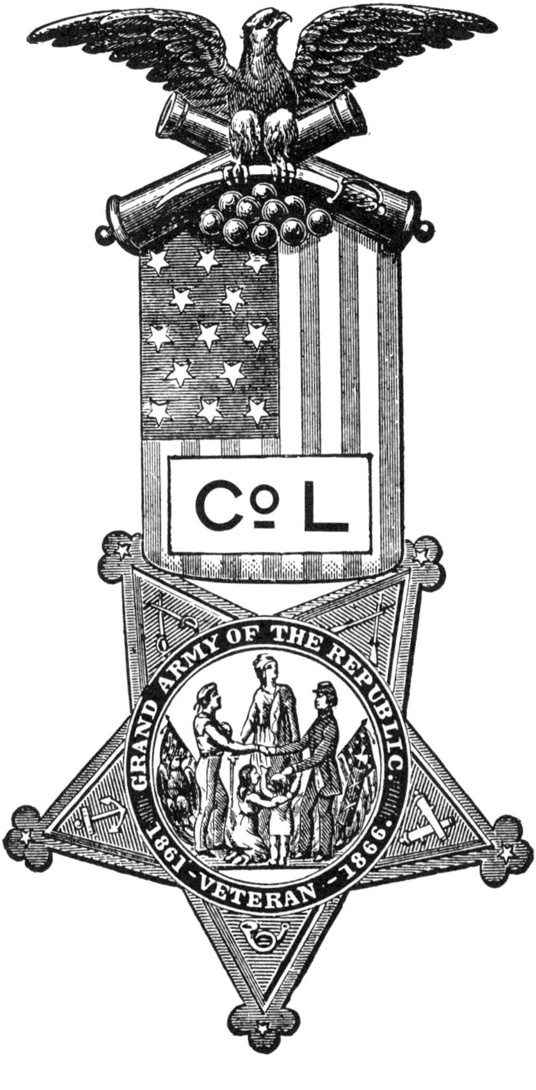
Co L
GRAND ARMY OF THE REPUBLIC
1861 · VETERAN · 1866

William Vincent Bowles,

Lieutenant Co. "L."

Born in the English Army about 1836; enlisted and served through the Crimea War in the English Army and honorably discharged.

Enlisted at Saginaw, Mich., April 13th, 1863, as Sergeant in Co. "L," 7th Michigan Cavalry; taken prisoner at Liberty Mills, Va., September 21st, 1863, and confined in Libby, Belle Isle, Andersonville and Millen Prisons; exchanged November 21st, 1864; promoted to Second Lieutenant May 24th, 1865; mustered out at Fort Leavenworth, Kansas, and honorably discharged.

ANDERSONVILLE.

As Composed by W. V. Bowles, 1st Sergt. Co. "L," 7th Mich., Cavalry When a Prisoner at Andersonville Prison, Ga.

In Georgia State, in Rebeldom now stands
'Midst pestilential air and swampy lands
A prison, a place more fit for Southern dogs,
That raised its lofty walls of pine wood logs.

A swamp lies in the center, it runs quite deep and wide,
Between two steep and sandy hills which slope on either side,
No house, or shed is to be seen within this dismal pen,
Wherein were thrust without remorse 30,000 Union men.

And in this dismal pen 'neath Heaven's blue vaulted sky,
With no other hope are left, to starve, to rot and die,
The aged man, the youth of tender years,
The maimed, the blind, the noble volunteers.

'Tis March, that month so windy and so cold,
Whose hoary frosts regard not young nor old,
It blights alike the sad, the strong man in his mirth,
And many a man before his time, consigned to Mother Earth.

Look on yonder group huddled 'round that little fire,
Ragged and shoeless, no hope doth them inspire,
See the lightning's flash, hark the thunder's roar,
While from the clouds above, the rain upon them pour.

The time is now midnight, the storm it has now ceased,
And many of these poor, helpless ones are from earthly cares released,
They are taken to the Dead Line, and there placed with the dead,
And early on the morrow will be laid in their last bed.

Alas! no wife or young one will be there to mourn and weep,
When departed worth is placed in earth to take death's quiet sleep,
But ignorant of the conditions that we are suffering here,
Is better for the happiness of those we hold so dear.

Who will bear the brunt of this great crying evil,
Is it Jefferson Davis, or his privy councillor, the Devil?
Or, shall the weight of it be laid upon,
Our paternal government—at Washington?

Time will tell, but what a recompense to all
The noble and the brave, who, at their country's call,
Surrendered homes and all with their valued lives thereafter,
Which they offered as a sacrifice upon their country's altar.

This is St. Patrick's Day, with stout hearts let us stand.
We will keep our courage up whilst in this region of the damned,
We will put our trust in Providence, whilst with grim death we cope,
Oh God, Oh God, whilst there is life there is hope.
—March 17, 1864.

STORY OF THE WAR.

"I have had many pleasant Christmas days," said State Land Agent James M. Page to a group of friends a few days ago, "but the Christmas I remember best was the most miserable day of my life. Tell you of it? Certainly, although it is a story that recalls days of bitter suffering, when life was worse than death, and yet of days that I would not care to forget altogether."

Mr. Page's friends drew up their chairs and prepared to listen.

"It was during the war in the early 60's," continued Mr. Page, "I was a member of Co. "A," 6th Michigan Cavalry, one of the Regiments of General Custer's famous Brigade. With twenty-three members of my Company, and Co. "L," 7th Michigan Cavalry, we were taken prisoners on the skirmish line near Orange Court House, Virginia, September 21st,

1863. We were taken to Libby Prison, where our Captain, who had been dangerously wounded, was paroled; that left twenty-two of us.

"Early in December we were taken to the notorious Belle Isle Prison, three miles above Richmond, on the James River, where 5,000 men were confined on about an acre of ground without blankets or shelter. Of all the prison hells of the South, this was undoubtedly the worst. It had the record for mortality from hunger and privation in proportion to the number confined.

"Eleven of us camped together, assisting each other all we could. A more royal band of young fellows I never met. The liveliest one of all the eleven was William V. Bowles, First Sergeant of Co. "L," 7th Michigan Cavalry. He was born and reared in the English Army. He was small in size, but big in heart, one of the most generous, jolly companions I ever knew.

"Christmas Day, 1863, came and with it a faint hope that a little of the sentiment, 'Peace on earth, good will to men' might prevail among our captors sufficient to induce them to give us a little additional allowance of corn bread or a pint of 'Nigger' pea soup, one of which was our daily portion. We were always hungry, but the gnawing at our stomachs seemed even worse than usual; was it not Christmas? The usual hour for issuing rations passed, but the pea soup didn't come. The time dragged by. In my mind I can even now see that gaunt, starving crowd of men as they stood around waiting for food that a self-respecting dog would refuse. At last we were told that the Commissary was too busy celebrating the day to get us anything to eat before the morrow.

"This was too much for Bowles. He cursed the "blasted Confederacy" from Jeff Davis down. Suddenly, after his indignation had somewhat subsided, he jumped to his feet and addressing the inseparable eleven, exclaimed:

" "Ere ye, you blooming, hungry Yanks, we are not to be swindled this way; hi ham going to hinvite you to a Christmas dinner we will have just as soon as we get into God's country once more." Then taking out his note book, he wrote the names of the eleven men comprising our squad. Next followed 'Bill of fare of the dinner that we did not get Christmas Day, 1863,' and it was an elaborate menu, too. I only remember a few of the items. There was plum pudding, turkey, oysters, and beef. It was his English idea of what a Christmas dinner ought to be. The very reading of it brought tears to the eyes of these starving men. We thought then that we would soon be exchanged or paroled and really expected to eat that dinner in the near future.

"Time went slowly on. The last of February, 1864, we were moved to Andersonville Prison, Georgia, where 35,000 Union soldiers were kept on less than 25 acres of ground during that summer and spring. One by one the men of our Company succumbed to the horrors of the place, until just Bowles and myself remained of the twenty-three young fellows who were captured on the skirmish line one year before. Sherman's Army drew near and all the prisoners were sent to Savannah, Charleston and other points. Bowles and I were moved to Savannah, then to Millen and on the 21st day of November, 1864, just fourteen months to a day from the time we were captured, we were exchanged and started up North.

"We were sights to behold, emaciated, ragged and dirty; we were the very picture of misery, and yet Bowles through it all had never lost heart and was the same jovial companion as in the days when our Brigade first took the field. After five days sailing we arrived at Annapolis, where we spent the week getting filled up, cleaned up and dressed up. Then we were given a furlough to go home to Michigan. Bowles was continually worrying about that Christmas dinner, and when we reached Baltimore nothing would do but that we must go to the best restaurant in the city and have it; and we did. The tables in the room were not large. 'Waiter,' ordered Bowles, 'we want a table set for eleven men, and give us the best service you 'ave.'

"I remonstrated with Bowles, but it was no use. 'This is the last tribute we can pay to those dead comrades and I am going to 'ave my way,' he said. Then with his memorandum book that was worn and black, he called off the names of our squad of eleven, only two of whom responded. Next, he read the bill of fare to the amazed waiter and ordered eleven dinners.

"Some time afterwards the head waiter came around and said, 'Your dinner is ready, but where are the rest of your company?' 'They're down South, dead,' was Bowles' reply.

"Then we sat down and were served to every dish that bill of fare contained. The eleven plates were filled at every course; it was the most remarkable Christmas dinner I ever ate. While our hearts were filled with thankfulness so far as we were personally concerned, our thoughts went back to the time, a year before, when our dead comrades and ourselves had stood about a Southern prison vainly praying for a pint of pea soup that was a prisoner's daily allowance. It was indeed a Christmas dinner that I shall never forget."

1863. 1901.

DAVID BIERD,

Sergeant Co. "L."

Carrollton, Saginaw Co., Mich.

Born at Manverse, Durham County, Ont., February 6th, 1845; enlisted at Saginaw, Saginaw County, Mich., March 17th, 1863, as Private in Co. "L," 7th Michigan Cavalry; was promoted to Corporal in March, 1864, Duty Sergeant in May, 1864, acted as First Sergeant from February 28th, 1865, promoted to First Sergeant April, 1865; mustered out at Salt Lake City, Utah, March 10th, 1866, and honorably discharged.

FIRST TIME UNDER FIRE.
By David Bierd.

Companies "L" and "M" joined the Regiment at Boonsboro, Md., July 8th, 1863.

On July 14th I was detailed to report at headquarters for duty. Picture in your mind a new recruit standing nearly six feet high and weighing less than 150 pounds, dressed in a uniform that would fit a man weighing two hundred pounds, looking for headquarters, and you will see a fair likeness of the writer, a recruit at the age of eighteen. On reaching headquarters I was directed to report to Colonel Litchfield as Orderly. When I found the Colonel and reported he looked me over and I fancied I could see a smile on his face as he took in my measurement. After examination he directed me to follow him, which I did for about eight months, or until he was taken prisoner on the Kilpatrick Raid around Richmond, March 1st, 1864.

In my first battle, "Falling Waters," the Regiment fully mounted, advanced along the side of a hill, but we did not go far before we were in range of the Rebel guns. As we were advancing their shells went flying over our heads, striking the ground in front of us and throwing dirt in our faces; this strange music of the shells and the excitement of the situation was new to me and so terrific that the Colonel with apprehension looked over his shoulder to see how his new Orderly was taking his medicine. We advanced but a few miles further when we encountered the Johnnies behind strong breastworks. The 6th Michigan made a charge and carried the works, losing a Major and a number of men; the 7th Michigan then moved as a support to their left; Major Granger, of our Regiment, with his Battalion being sent to our right. He then advanced between the 6th and the 7th, having dismounted part of his command and drove the enemy from the field. Our Regiment was then divided, part going to support the skirmishers and the rest to the support of Battery "M." An order was given for the portion of the Regiment supporting Battery "M" to charge; Colonel Mann turned to Colonel Litchfield and said, "You lead the charge and I will see what the General wants." Colonel Litchfield then gave the order, "Draw sabres! Forward, Charge!" and turned to me and said, "If my horse is killed or wounded go to the rear and hurry forward to me another one." You can imagine how green I was when I had to inquire of him where I would find the rear.

With less than one hundred men in line, with Colonel Litchfield in the lead, we charged down a lane in column of fours, with the Johnnies in a field on our left, and in an orchard on our right. On coming out of the lane and up onto a small rise of ground where stood an old log house, we were more than surprised to find in view from three to four thousand Rebel Infantry, not more than ten rods in our front. At this point Colonel Litchfield, with his sabre above his head, roared out with a voice of thunder, "Down with your guns, every mother's son of you!" and all you could see were the hands and hats of the Rebels waving frantically in the air. When the Colonel took time to look around all he could see were two men, Captain Sargeant of Co. "H" and myself, the balance of the Regiment were busy caring for over four hundred prisoners they had taken. Our position on the hill getting too hot we fell back and were kept on the skirmish line the remainder of the day.

This is a rough account of what I saw and heard in my first day's fight and battle.

1865.

Reuben N. Ormsby,

Co. "L."

Armada, Mich.

Born in Livonia Township, Wayne County, Mich., February 11th, 1843; enlisted at Pontiac, Oakland County, Mich., February 3rd, 1865, as Private in Co. "L," 7th Michigan Cavalry; detailed as Adjutant's Clerk by Adjutant Charles O. Pratt, May 20th, 1865; mustered out at Fort Leavenworth, Kansas, December 10th, 1865, and honorably discharged.

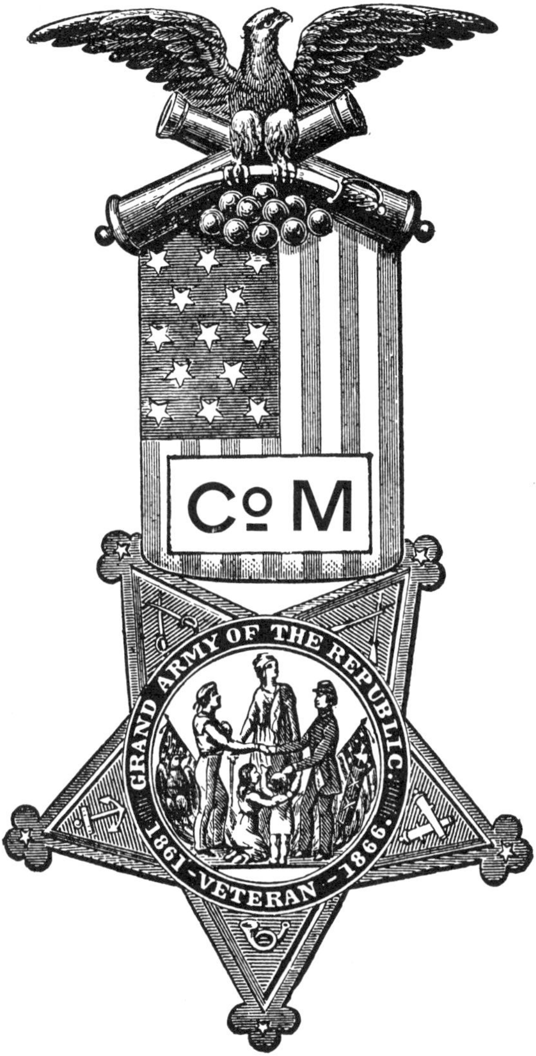
Co M
GRAND ARMY OF THE REPUBLIC
1861 - VETERAN - 1866

1865.

JAMES B. LOOMIS,
Captain Co. "M."
Nome, Alaska.

Born at Ypsilanti, Washtenaw Co., Mich., April 11th, 1839; enlisted at Battle Creek, Mich., September 4th, 1862, as Sergeant in Co. "A," 7th Michigan Cavalry; promoted to Sergeant Major May 1st, 1863, First Lieutenant August 1st, 1863; Captain, May 24th, 1865; mustered out at Fort Leavenworth, Kansas, December 15th, 1865, and honorably discharged.

1864.   1901.

JOHN B. MASTEN,
First Lieutenant Co. "M."
Adrian, Lenawee Co., Mich.

Born January 7th, 1836, at Sparta, Livingston County, N. Y.; enlisted at Raisin, Lenawee County, Mich., December 9th, 1862, as private in Co. "I," 7th Michigan Cavalry; was promoted to Sergeant January 15th, 1863, and to Second Lieutenant August 16th, 1864, to First Lieutenant May 24th, 1865, and transferred to 1st Michigan Veteran Cavalry November 17th, 1865; mustered out at Salt Lake City, Utah Ter., March 10th, 1866, and honorably discharged.

1865　　　　　　　　　　　1901

WILLIAM O. LEE,

Quartermaster Sergeant Co. "M."

379 Hancock Ave. East, Detroit, Mich.

Born November 17th, 1844, in Arbela Township, Tuscola County, Mich.; enlisted at Saginaw, E. S., Saginaw County, Mich., February 14th, 1864, as private in Co. "M," 7th Michigan Cavalry; promoted to Corporal June 15th, 1865, and detailed to act as Quartermaster Sergeant of Co. "M;" promoted to Quartermaster Sergeant August 15th, 1865; mustered out at Fort Leavenworth, Kansas, December 7th, 1865, and honorably discharged.

DISAPPOINTMENTS.
By Wm. O. Lee.

Well do we all remember the surrender at Appomattox, and afterwards the northward march doing reconstruction duty, reaching Alexandria on the 19th of May, 1865, where the mounted and unmounted of our Regiment once more joined forces, and on the 20th marched from Alexandria to Washington by way of the famous long bridge; going into camp on the outskirts of the Capital City; the Grand Review on the 22d and 23d of May; Governor Crapo's visit to our camp, and his assurance that we were going home; and our boarding a train of cattle cars that were to transport us to the glorious North and our pleasant homes.

Then followed disappointment after disappointment. The next morning after leaving Washington we awakened to find ourselves at Harper's Ferry and speeding South and West instead of at Baltimore and northward towards our homes. Disappointment when we arrived and left Parkersburg, W. Va., steaming down the Ohio River past Cincinnati and Louisville, rounding Cairo, up the Mississippi River, past St. Louis, and up the Missouri River, past Jefferson City to Fort Leavenworth, Kansas, where we landed on June 6th.

Disappointment to those whose time had or was about to expire, that they were not mustered out and allowed to go home; and to the balance that they were not getting their pay for services rendered, nor informed of their future and destination.

Disappointment when on the morning of the 24th of June we were ordered to horse and saddle, and started on our westward march across the barren plains, and through a country infested with hostile bands of Indians, to where, no one knew, nor could we find out; when on July 28th we reached Fort Collins in the Rocky Mountains. From there on we continued our westward march detailing men from our ranks and leaving them at each station as we passed, constantly depleting our numbers until the 6th of August, Co. "M" reached Sulphur Spring Station, N. D., our western post.

Disappointment at delay of specific information from the War Department as to our final disposition.

Disappointment on October 5th, when an order from the War Department was received, ordering a portion of our command to return East to be mustered out, while a part of the command was ordered to remain in the service and march farther West.

Disappointment to those returning East when at Denver, Col., on the 30th of October, with a foot of snow on the ground, we were ordered to turn in our horses, equipment and ordnance, and start on a march of nearly seven hundred miles on foot, through the enemy's country in the dead of winter.

Disappointment when we reached Fort Leavenworth on December 3d and found that we were not to be mustered out until we reach Michigan.

Disappointment when we were mustered out to find that the Government compelled us to pay our own transportation from Denver to Fort Leavenworth, and upon that point we have been disappointed ever since.

But with all our disappointments we felt to thank God when we received our spread-eagles in the form of a discharge as a permit from the Government admitting that we were once more free men at liberty to wander as we choose, and free from military orders and military dictations.

1863.   1902.

John F. Simpson,

Sergeant Co. "M."

Grand Ledge, Mich.

Born at Pine Woods, Madison County, N. Y., March 13th, 1845; enlisted at Ionia, Ionia County, Mich., December 16th, 1861, as Private in Co. "I," 1st Berdans U. S. Sharp Shooters; mustered out at Baltimore, Md., September 15th, 1862, and honorably discharged.

Enlisted at Ionia, Ionia County, Mich., June 11th, 1863, as Sergeant in Co. "M," 7th Michigan Cavalry; taken prisoner at Morton's Ford, Va., December 28th, 1863, and was confined at Libby, Belle Isle, Andersonville, and Millen prisons; paroled at Savannah, Ga., November 20th, 1864; exchanged January 1st, 1865; joined the Regiment May 1st, 1865; mustered out at Salt Lake City, Utah, March 10th, 1866, and honorably discharged.

ANDERSONVILLE.

By John F. Simpson.

At eight o'clock on the night of January 1st, 1864, known as "the cold New Year's," I registered at Libby Prison in Richmond, Va.

Although it was thirty-eight years ago, I can remember nearly every one of the poor starved faces of the little contingent of the 7th Michigan Cavalry who crowded around me to learn the news from the front and to tell the horrors of that dreadful place.

After a sojourn of eleven months in various Rebel prisons, I give it as my opinion that there never was (nor never will be) another such place of confinement as Andersonville. The original enclosure of nineteen acres was established in an unbroken woods, and the timber was only removed as it was wanted for the necessities of the prison. The enclosure was made in January, 1864, and enlarged during the summer to twenty-five acres, being a quadrangle of 1,285 feet by 865 feet. The greatest length was from north to south, the ground rising from the center towards each end in rather a steep, rounded hill; the northern one being the highest and of the greatest extent.

A small stream ran across it through a narrow valley filled with a compost washed down by the rains. The stockade was formed of pine logs twenty feet in length and about eight to ten inches in diameter, sunk five feet in the ground and placed close together. Within the interior space, at a distance of seventeen feet from the stockade, ran the "dead line," marked by small posts and a narrow strip of pine boards nailed on the tops of them. The gates, of which there were two, were on the west side of the stockade, enclosing a space of thirty feet square, "more or less," protected by massive doors at either end. They were arranged and swung on the principal of canal locks.

Upon the stockade were fifty-two sentry boxes, raised above the tops of the palisades and accessible to the guards by ladders. In these stood fifty-two guards with loaded arms and so near that they could converse with each other. In addition to these were several forts mounted with field artillery commanding the fatal space and its masses of perishing men. Even after the lapse of so many years I hardly dare to recall the terrible scenes I witnessed in that cruel, unrelenting place. Of the long months of starvation when one knew neither shelter nor protection from the changeable skies above, nor the pitiless, unfeeling earth beneath. Think of thirty thousand men penned in by a closed stockade upon twenty-five acres of ground, from which every tree and shrub had been uprooted for fuel to cook our scanty food, huddled like cattle without shelter or blankets, half clad and hungry, with the dreary night setting in after a day of autumn rain. The high ground would not hold us all, the valley was filled with the swollen brook, while seventeen feet from the stockade ran the fatal dead line, beyond which no man might step and live.

With the mingling of over thirty thousand men, composed of all elements, there is always bound to be many of the bad, especially when hunger and starvation stares them in the face; such was the case in Andersonville, and by them pillaging and even murder was being committed. Such depredations had grown to alarming proportions and the better element proposed to hunt out the guilty parties and make an example of them. With that end in view, the prison was policed, arrests made and guilty parties convicted and punished, and as evidence of the fact I herewith make a copy of my diary as kept at that time:

"July 11th, 1864.—This has been the greatest day of my prison life. The whole camp of over 30,000 men has been in an excited turmoil since early morning. The six condemned 'Raiders' were executed to-day. About twenty-five of the gang were taken outside a week ago by permission of Captain Wirz and were given a fair trial by our own men, First Sergeant O. W. Carpenter of Co. "M," 7th Michigan Cavalry, acting as Judge Advocate. The six men hung to-day were all known to have robbed and murdered helpless comrades. Their names are William Collins, alias Mosby, Co. "D," 88th Pennsylvania; John Sarsfield, 144th New York; Charles Curtis, Battery "A," 5th Rhode Island Artillery; Pat Delaney, 83rd Pennsylvania; A. Munn, U. S. Navy, and W. R. Rickson, U. S. Navy.

"They were brought into camp about ten o'clock by Captain Wirz and turned over to our police squad under command of 'Limber Jim,' who superintended the hanging. Father Hamilton, a Catholic Priest, accompanied them to the scaffold. Curtis, who got his arms freed, made a break for liberty, but was soon run down and brought back, when the six were assisted to mount the scaffold and placed in a row, all standing on the one plank. All were given a chance to talk and with the exception of Rickson took advantage of the opportunity. Munn, a fine looking fellow in Marine dress, said that starvation with evil companions had made him what he was. He spoke of his mother and sisters in New York and said the sad news that would be carried home to them made him want to curse God that he had ever been born. Delaney said he would rather be hung than live here, as the most of them had to live, on their allowance of rations. He bid us all good-bye and said his name was not Delaney, therefore his friends would never know his fate, his Andersonville history dying with him.

"At a signal from 'Limber Jim' the plank was knocked from under them and we saw them change from strong men to dangling heaps of clothes. The rope broke with Collins and he begged hard for his life, but it was all in vain, and he was soon swinging with the rest.

"The death rate is increasing rapidly and is now over one

hundred every day, mostly from scurvy and starvation, and this on only twenty-five acres of ground."

What did we do? Need you ask. Where did we go? God only knew. For on the face of this whole green earth there was no place for us but that circumscribed twenty-five acres. It has been said that history repeats itself, but I am assured in my own mind that the horrors inflicted by that monster "Wirz" and the sufferings endured by the 12,920 helpless Union priosoners who starved to death at Andersonville will never be duplicated. Among them are the following members of my own Regiment:

Co. A.
O'Brien, William H.
Springer, Joseph
Co. B.
Hartsell, George
Jakeway, Ebenezer
McCaughn, William
Whittaker, Joseph F.
Co. C.
Clago, Stephen
Fredenburg, Benj. F.
Honsinger, Walter L.
Jagnet, E. B.
Parks, Van Rensaler
Parmalee, Joseph
Schermerhorn, John
Way, Thomas H.
Co. D.
Gibbs, Joseph S.
Grant, Anson H.
Hale, Samuel B.
Hance, Charles
McArthur, Wallace
Pettibone, Salem E.
Sprague, Benjamin
Co. E.
Arseno, William H.
Daily, Almerick
Findlater, Hugh
Keating, Michael
Lowell, James
Simonds, Barlow H.

Simonds, Albert O.
Co. F.
Blanchard, James
Cooper, John F.
Cruice, John D.
Howe, Isaac O.
Riley, Miles
Stewart, Clark
Miller, L.
Co. G.
Bennett, Irwin
Johnson, Luman H.
Co. H.
McClary, W. H.
McClure, Ralph
Smith, Perry W.
Co. I.
Jackson, James
Mosher, Stephen L.
Parsons, Zenas
Co. K.
Springer, J.
Tracy, Dori
Tubbs, Philip
Wright, William A.
Co. L.
Deas, Abraham
Mason, Peter
Smith, William
Co. M.
Barnard, G.
Smith, William

1866.

HARRIS G. DOWNS,

Corporal Co. "M."

Dead.

Born at Tuscola, Tuscola County, Mich., May 8th, 1844; enlisted as private in Co. "M," 7th Michigan Cavalry, March 20th, 1863; promoted to Corporal of Co. "M" June, 1865; mustered out at Salt Lake City, Utah, March 10th, 1866, and honorably discharged. Died from the effects of a fractured knee from being thrown from a horse in Madison County, Mont., April 26th, 1869.

1864. 1901.

THOS. C. WILLIAMS,
Corporal Co. "M."
Hastings, Mich.

Born March 28th, 1840, at Euclid, Cuyahoga County, O.; enilsted at Grand Rapids, Mich., June 9th, 1863, as private in Co. "M," 7th Michigan Cavalry; was promoted to Corporal June, 1865; mustered out at Salt Lake City, Utah Ter., March 10th, 1866, and honorably discharged.

1901.

DUANE WILLITT,

Co. "M."

Vassar, Mich.

Born at Theresa, Jefferson County, N. Y., June 5th, 1844; enlisted at Tuscola, Tuscola County, Mich., March 20th, 1863, as private in Co. "M," 7th Michigan Cavalry; mustered out at Washington, D. C., November 16th, 1865, and honorably discharged.

1901.

ORANGE A. JUBB,

Co. "M."

Nunica, Ottawa Co., Mich.

Born August 27th, 1839, in Ingham County, Mich.; enlisted at Nunica, Ottawa County, Mich., April 1, 1863, as private in Co. "M," 7th Michigan Cavalry; was wounded at Sheppardstown, Va., August 25th, 1864, and lost left leg below the knee; was mustered out at Detroit, Mich., August 14th, 1865, and honorably discharged.

WHEN I LOST MY LEG.

By Orange A. Jubb.

I was wounded at Sheppardstown on the 25th day of August, 1864, about 3 o'clock in the afternoon.

Our Regiment had been in the advance since early in the morning and it must have been about 10 a. m. when we were stopped by an overwhelming force of the Johnnies. We fought and held them at bay for about two hours, when we had to retreat. During that time I had shot sixty shots and had the last round of my cartridges in my carbine. I think I had shot two Johnnies, when in a charge in a cornfield I was hit by a minnie ball in my left leg below the knee. You all remember that cornfield; if you do not, I do, and always will.

I went to Captain Carpenter after I was wounded, as he was then acting as Major, and told him that I was wounded. He asked me if it was bad. I told him that my leg was broken, and he said to James Doyle, "Take Jubb's arms and go with him to the rear," which he did. Major Drew advised us to keep in the rear of the battery until we found the rear.

About that time our boys succeeded in breaking the rebel line and the Brigade started for Sheppardstown Ford, where the balance of the Cavalry Corps were. Our Brigade had been cut off from the others and they were fighting near Sheppardstown. I and some more wounded took the road for Harper's Ferry, also some that were dismounted and some that were not who went along with us. I think about 200 in all. We got to Harper's Ferry about 11 o'clock that night. I rode my horse all the way except about one mile, when I rode in an ambulance.

When the ball struck my leg it was numb and did not pain me for about an hour; after that it pained me fearfully. It does not hurt to be shot, but the after-collapse is the terror. My leg was amputated about midnight, August 25th.

I remained at Harper's Ferry until the last of September; was then moved to Pleasant Valley, from there to Fredericksburg, Md., and from there to Detroit, where I was discharged on the 14th day of August, 1865.

My leg is in such a condition that I cannot wear an artificial leg, so have to use a peg leg, and will have to peg it all the days of my life.

1863.

FRANKLIN ROBINSON,

Co. "M."

Dead.

Born March 15th, 1842, at Robinson, Ottawa County, Mich.; enlisted at Robinson, Ottawa County, Mich., April 20th, 1863, as private in Co. "M," 7th Michigan Cavalry; was mustered out at Detroit September 21st, 1865, and honorably discharged.

1901.

CHARLES W. LOOMIS,

Co. "M."

Ivy P. O., Saginaw Co., Mich.

Born June 13th, 1846, at Watertown, Jefferson County, N. Y.; enlisted at Grand Haven, Mich., April, 1863, as private in Co. "M," 7th Michigan Cavalry; was wounded in reconnoisance on east bank of Rapidan River, in Virginia while on detached service with Battery "K," 1st U. S. Regular Light Artillery, some time in the Autumn of 1863; was mustered out at Philadelphia, Penn., July 5th, 1865, and honorably discharged.

1901.

GEORGE R. PERRY,

Co. "M."

St. Johns, Mich.

Born at Colton, St. Lawrence County, N. Y., October 14th, 1846; enlisted at Maple Rapids, Clinton County, Mich., June 6th, 1863, as Private in Co. "M," 7th Michigan Cavalry; wounded in right shoulder on the 1st of April at the Battle of Five Forks; mustered out at Detroit, Mich., September 2nd, 1865, and honorably discharged.

THE DAUGHTER OF THE REGIMENT

1892
MRS. EMMA MANN VYNNE,
Care of "The Smart Set." 452 Fifth Ave., New York, N. Y.
Daughter of Col. W. D. Mann.
Elected to the Regiment October 19th, 1900.

THE BABY

1902.
RITA MARY LEE.
Born August 2d, 1896.
Daughter of Wm. O. and Rose Vail Lee,
379 Hancock Ave. E., Detroit, Mich.

APPENDIX.

"ROLL OF HONOR"

CONTAINING THE NAMES OF MEMBERS OF THE SEVENTH MICHIGAN
VOLUNTEER CAVALRY, WHO LOST THEIR LIVES IN BATTLE,
DIED OF WOUNDS AND DISEASE, AND IN REBEL PRISONS
DURING THE WAR OF THE REBELLION AND A
PARTIAL LIST SO FAR AS KNOWN OF
THOSE WHO HAVE DIED
SINCE THE WAR AS

COMPILED BY DR. ASA B. ISHAM,
Late First Lieutenant of Company "F."

Taken from "THE HISTORY OF THE SEVENTH MICHIGAN CAVALRY" as compiled by LIEUTENANT J. Q. A. SESSIONS, late of Company "D," and from the "RECORDS OF THE SEVENTH MICHIGAN CAVALRY ASSOCIATION."

ABSENT MEMBERS.

Address of Dr. Asa B. Isham, Oct. 11, 1901.

I acknowledge a sort of retributive justice in calling upon me to answer for the absent members, *in as much* as I have been more conspicuous by my absence than by my presence in years past; not as a matter of choice upon my part, but, arising out of the necessities of one who has to labor for his daily bread. Every one with any soul in him must regret to miss these meetings. At least to me they are an inspiration, and after each one I attend I return to my daily duties with a greater feeling of satisfaction in the reflection that I hold membership in a body of men of distinguished merit. To one moved by this sentiment of the worth of his old associates this gathering has an attraction, it constitutes for the time being the center of his mental vision. He strains the ear, perchance to catch a word of Crane's polished oratory, of Colonel Briggs' keen wit, of President Lee's happy hits, of the drolleries escaping from the lips of Captain Fisher, of a note of Wescott's melody, now, alas, hushed forever; or, a morsel of the weighty wisdom that wells up through the tall forms of Chaplain Nash and Lieutenant Sessions. And when a listener becomes very intent the mouth commonly gapes open and becomes parched. It is in order then to moisten it and the moistening may have to be repeated at frequent intervals. When, therefore, late at night, the "absent member" presents himself to his spouse, quite moist and limp, the inquiry is natural upon her part as to what may have caused his condition. A Regimental Reunion away off in Kalamazoo or Detroit may seem to the good woman a very remote explanation; but there are mysteries that even the brightest of us fail to grasp.

You may depend upon it that the absent members bear us in mind to-night. The true soldier is ever responsive to the ties of comradeship, and you may rest assured that the living absent members will come in, as occasion permits, to renew the bond of "blood brotherhood."

But there are absent ones who never yet have met with us in this Association and whom we shall never greet again upon this side of the dark river. Three hundred and fifty of our best comrades fell upon the field of battle, died of wounds, or were starved to death in Rebel prisons during the progress of the war.

Such men as:

Lieutenant Colonel Melvin Brewer
Major Henry W. Granger

Co. A.

Adams, Oscar H.
Alexander, Samuel
Brickell, Edward J.
Brownell, Horace
Chappell, Chester C.
Dumphrey, Edwin
Heinck, John
Knapp, Charles C.
Lang, Edward S.
Lingo, Daniel
Luke, J. W.
Matchett, Noel
O'Brien, William H.
Park, John
Parks, Allen C.
Pierce, Sidney S.
Shafer, Charles F.
Springer, Joseph R.
Strong, George W.
Walter, Nelson
Wilcox, Charles
Worthen, George A.

Co. B.

Austin, Stephen
Baker, George
Fisher, Mathias
Hager, John S.
Hartsell, George
Haskins, James
Hicks, Hamilton
Jakeway, Ebenezer
Keller, Henry H.
Laird, William J.
Larrue, Hiram J.
Long, Edward
McCaughn, William
Perkins, Myron H.
Russel, Jason
Stearns, William A.
Whittaker, Joseph F.

Co. C.

Barnhart, Martin
Case, Silas D.
Church, Benjamin
Clago, Stephen
Cook, Elliott A.
Deihl, Henry
Fredenburg, B. F.
Heminger, Isaac
Hill, John
Honsinger, Walter
Jagnet, E. B.
Kelliher, Maurice
Miller, Jacob L.
McComber, William
Parks, Van Rensaler
Parmelee, Joseph
Schermerhorn, John
Smith, Charles
Way, Thomas H.

Co. D.

Adams, William H.
Bush, Christian
Bush, Fredrick
Compau, Peter
Fordham, Albert
Gibbs, Joseph H.
Gilbert, George W.
Grant, Anson H.
Haines, Henry
Hale, Samuel B.
Hance, Charles
Hartland, H. P.
Jackson, Orlando D.
Karcher, Johiel
Mason, George I.
McArthur, Wallace

Milburn, John
Pettibone, Salem E.
Sprague, Benjamin
Thompson, Henry
Vaness, George E.

Co. E.
Arseno, William H.
Croman, William
Daily, Almerick
Finch, Charles O.
Finch, Robert
Findlater, Hugh
Hopkins, Horace
House, Barnum B.
Keating, Michael.
Kisner, Samuel
Lowell, James
McLain, Alexander
Nay, Harmon
Robinson, James B.
Simonds, Albert O.
Simonds, Barlow H.
Smith, Thomas

Co. F.
Armstrong, James H.
Bedel, Harlan
Bedel, James T.
Blanchard, James
Cochran, Harlan
Cooper, John F.
Cruice, John D.
Guio, Henry
Hoag, Robert
Howe, Isaac O.
Lundy, George W.
Mercer, Thomas
Miller, L.
Minor, Charles E.
Page, Truman
Paule, Jacob
Ralph, Oscar O.
Riley, Miles
Stewart, Clark T.
Wilson, Royal S.

Co. G.
Bennett, Irwin
Churchill, Alfred W.
Crampton, T. H.
Delamater, Martin R.
Johnson, Luman H.
Motley, Thomas
Spear, Truman

Co. H.
Knapp, Vine
McClary, William H.
McClure, Ralph
Mills, Harvey
Nichols, William H.
Reasoner, Henry M.
Smith, Perry W.
Stewart, John
Woodard, Henry J.

Co. I.
Cochran, William J.
Hasty, Robert
Jackson, James
Mosher, Stephen L.
Nolan, Arthur D.
Parsons, Zenas
Williams, Squire

Co. K.
Baker, Daniel
Downer, Jacob R.
Dunn, Daniel
England, Morris
Hamel, Herman or Harrison
Ingledue, Eber
Isham, George
McDonald, John J.
Smith, Eli
Springer, J.
Tracy, David
Tubbs, Philip
Wright, William A.

Co. L.
Mead, Lieutenant Joseph L.
Bates, William F.
Brown, William
Cameron, Daniel
Coombs, John G.
Dees, Abraham
Green, Albert A.
Hooker, Alonzo H.
Johnson, Henry
Mayfield, Henry
Mason, Peter
Pattison, Henry
Pomeroy, David H.
Rammont, John
Rolling, Charles D.
Siel, David
Smith, William
Terry, George A.
Thompson, Thomas D.

Wilson, John
Wright, Ephriam
    Co. M.
Carver, Lieutenant Lucius
Austin, Francis
Barnard, G.
Carpenter, Otis W.
Durham, Emery
Fox, C. A.

Fox, William H.
Gunner, James
Hawkins, Alphonzo
Perkins, Henry
Perkinson, George
Quirk, John
Smith, William
Taber, Winfield S.
Van Duzer, Charles E.

Fully a thousand more have passed away, during and since the war, of disease, and, in consequence of wounds received in action. It is manifestly impossible to name them all, but among them are:

Major John L. Huston
Major L. F. Warner
Major Alexander Walker
Surgeon William Upjohn
Surgeon George R. Richards
    Co. A.
Bradley, Randall P.
Briminstool, Alonzo
Clark, Edgar A.
Collins, Joseph
Fulton, David
Hogan, Patrick
Lowry, Alexander
Marcott, Oliver
Millman, Samuel
Sayers, Nathan S.
Schrowder, Michael
Smith, Alonzo D.
Stanton, Charles W.
Taylor, Ezekiel
Trumble, James
Walling, Pitts J.
Welton, George A.
    Co. B.
Gray, Lieutenant Elliott
Bridleman, George W.
Hill, Albert W.
Howard, Andrew
Jordon, James N.
Nincy, Henry
Safford, Josiah
Seymour, Wilson B.
Van Pelt, Francis H.
    Co. C.
Hamlin, Captain John H.
Crocker, Lieutenant Erastus B.
Holton, Lieuteant Charles M.

Belden, H. S.
Hunter, W. W.
Knowles, William H.
Morton, Robert
Sherman, Nelson
Trumbal, Simeon E.
Van Voorhees, William
    Co. D.
Birney, Captain James G.
Benham, Elias P.
Chandler, Horace
Clark, Lafayette F.
Gladding, Onslow
    Co. G.
Ferris, Lieutenant George
Hill, Lieutenant George W.
Bates, J. D.
Bell, William
Chappel, Enoch
Dice, Francis
Henderson, George
Ipe, John
North, Charles
Philips, George S.
Tibbitts, Howard A.
    Co. H.
Douglas, Captain Richard
Sergeant, Captain David
Clark, Lieutenant Franklin B.
Dunnett, Lieutenant D. W.
Andrus, Henry
Batt, James A.
Briggs, John E.
Clark, James
Fisher, Albert H.
Kemp, Alfred
Kent, Theodore F.

Martin, Eugene W.
Mason, Charles
Mingo, James H.
Norwood, ——
Palmer, John L.
Prentice, Sidney R.
Richards, William H.
Rowley, William H.
Russell, James F.
Shean, William
Smith, Stephen D.
   Co. I.
Clark, Captain John A.
Littlefield, Lieutenant Daniel
Bennett, Reuben
Cornell, Samuel
Dreifenbacher, Andrew
Fairchilds, James
Fish, Austin O.
Gardner, William
Gay, Newton S.
Hall, Lorinus A.
Harris, George
Grisler, Charles
Hartson, Henry N.
Hammil, M. V.
Hawkins, Joseph N.
Herring, Willis W.
Holmes, W. I.
Howe, George W.
Lindsay, Wallace
Marsh, Oliver
Preston, E. A.
Pickett, Orange
Price, William
Smoke, Abram
Traver, Bushnell
Turner, David
Vroman, David
Whitcomb, Orin J.
   Co. E.
Willits, Captain Wellington
Andrews, Charles
Bolton, William C.
Case, Paul
Davenport, John
Higby, Elisha J.
Joslyn, Rudolphus
King, Vincent
Lee, Chauncey L.
Loomis, Augustus S.
Luther, C. L.
Meech, Charles K.
Monroe, William

Parmeter, Orville
Palmer, William H.
Whitman, Hiram
   Co. F.
Dodge, Lieutenant Winchester T.
Lyon, Lieutenant Charles
Blodgett, Jay
Cain, Russel A.
Fritts, Alvin W.
Hoagland, Abram
Johnson, Charles
Kelly, William J.
Lewis, Edward F.
Mellon, Jerome
Peck, John W.
Robinson, George H.
Philips, Peleg T.
Stowe, Simeon
Williams, Job J.
Henderson, Charles
Jones, Josiah W.
Lewis, J.
Lucas, Charles H.
McDale, John R.
McLoud, John
Polmanteer, S. A.
Shepherd, Perry
Sommers, John
Wescott, Andrew
Wood, John
   Co. K.
Moore, Captain Heman N.
Bennett, Nelson
Boswell, Abram
Cline, Andrew J.
Livermore, Henry H.
Lowe, Henry
Madison, Joseph
Rankin, Peter A.
Reed, Henry A.
Robinson, Franklin
Spencer, James L.
Stanwell, James O.
Stilwell, James O.
   Co. L.
Carll, Lieutenant Samuel B.
Baird, Henry C.
Benson, Stephen E.
Brenen, Michael
Gates, George W.
Gates, Henry J.
Marshall, Richard
Mosher, Charles
Smith, John

Co. M.
Gregg, Lieutenant Riley A.
Munson, Lieutenant Henry P.
Brannan, M.
Cofman, John
Coates, L.

Fisher, Albert
Gifford, George R.
Riggs, E. R.
Sprague, William P.
Sickles, Josiah R.
Steucke, Henry

The small minority remaining is crowding hard upon those departed, so that, "One doth tread upon another's heels so fast they follow." These Comrades, through their noble patriotism, have glorified humanity, exalted the Nation, and enrolled themselves among the blessed. We cherish their memories, they are enshrined in our hearts, and, we would not recall them if we could.

"We will not weep for them who died so well,
But we will gather 'round the hearth and tell
The story of their lives."

And the story will disclose that, in the hot fires of battle they welded a tottering Republic into a mighty Nation, for the deliverance from tyranny of millions upon millions of beings in two hemispheres, as well also as for the uplifting of all people everywhere. But for the "absent ones," and you, my comrades, gathered here to-night, who sustained and bore it up from 1862 to 1865, "Old Glory" would not have been the unequivocal symbol of liberty, union and strength that it is to-day, as it grandly floats, an object of reverence at home and of respect everywhere abroad.

Our "absent ones," as well as those present, belong to the immortals referred to in the sublime words of the great Lincoln at Gettysburg, "The brave men, living and dead, who struggled here have consecrated it far beyond our power to add or detract; the world will little note, nor long remember, what we say here, but it can never forget what they did here."

INDEX

PICTURES, PERSONALS AND COMPANIES

NAME.	NO. OF PICTURES.	PAGE.
Anthony, Henry L.	2	96
Appendix		302
Armstrong, Capt. Geo. A.	2	154
Baby, The		301
Barden, William C.	2	246
Barnes, E. W.	2	268
Beardslee, Clark H.		234
Bellingar, George W.	2	266
Bellinger, R. Marshall	2	98
Bierd, David	2	277
Birney, Capt. James G.	2	157
Bowles, Lieut. William V.		272
Briggs, Col. George G.	2	34
Carpenter, Major James L.	2	55
Carver, Lieut. Lucius		89
Clark, Lieut. Frank B.		254
Cobb, George P.	2	188
Company "A"		85
Company "B"		111
Company "C"		121
Company "D"		153
Company "E"		195
Company "F"		219
Company "G"		243
Company "H"		253
Company "I"		261
Company "K"		267
Company "L"		271
Company "M"		281
Cook, Elliott A.		133
Crane, Albert	2	208
Crossett, Corydon		187
Custer, General George A.		17

NAME.	NO. OF PICTURES.	PAGE.
Darling, Lt. Col. Daniel H.	2	46
Daughter of the Regiment.		300
DeGraff, Lieut. Henry.		78
Dobson, George W.	2	179
Doherty, Joseph		235
Downs, Harris		292
Ferris, Lieut. George		228
Fisher, Captain William H.	2	86
Fisher, William		255
Gage, William Glover.	2	128
Genney, David G.	2	211
Granger, Major Henry W.		51
Grant, General U. S.		12
Gray. Lieut. Elliott.		112
Griffin, Bartholomew	2	122
Hastings, Lieut. William.		262
Havens, Lieut. Edwin R.	2	90
Helmer, Albert M.	2	151
Hibbard, W. H.		250
Hill, Lieut. George W.	2	244
Holmes, Capt. R. H.	2	196
Hoover, William H.	2	137
House, William E.	2	116
Hulce, Benj.		264
Hunt, Oscar I.		105
Hustler, Charles		142
Isham, Lieut. Asa B.	2	223
Jubb, Orange A.		295
Kenfield, William F.	2	238
Kilpatrick, General H. J.		15
Lee, Rita Mary.		301
Lee, William O.	2	284
Lincoln, Pres. Abraham.		10
Litchfield, Col. A. C.	2	27
Longman, Arthur	2	257
Loomis, Charles W.		298
Loomis, Capt. James B.		282
Lyon, Major Farnham	2	64
Mann, Capt. Stephen B.	2	220
Mann, Col. William D.	2	20-21
Masten, Lieut. John B.	2	283
McCormick, Capt. George W.	2	202

310

NAME.	NO. OF PICTURES.	PAGE.
McDonald, John L.	2	107
McNaughton, Lieut. Daniel	2	73
Milbourn, Frank	2	181
Monument	1	VII.
Nash, Chaplain Charles P.		71
Newcomb, Major George K.		50
Olmstead, Albert H.		183
Ormsby, Reuben N.		280
Perry, George R.		299
Perry, Oliver H.	2	134
Pollard, William H.		175
Pray, Andrew	2	170
Raymond, Walden W.		209
Robinson, Frank		297
Rock, James L.	2	146-147
Rose, David B.		124
Russell, Edwin O.		184
Sessions, Lieut. J. Q. A.	2	160
Shafer, Dr. Marion A.		81
Sheridan, Gen. Phil. H.		14
Shotwell, Albert	2	167
Simpson, John F.	2	287
Smith, Lieut. Harmon		229
Smith, James		123
Space, Nathan H.		236
Sproul, Major Robert	2	52
Streeter, Raymond T.		102
Thomas, Lieut. Henry F.		113
Tubbs, Lieut. Butler S.		245
Vynne, Mrs. Emma Mann		300
Von Daniels, Ernest		143
Watson, George W.	2	216
Weston, Dr. Adelbert H.	2	114
White, Charles P.	2	232
Willett, Duane		294
Williams, Thomas C.	2	293
Wilson, Rev. John N.	2	138

INDEX

HISTORICAL SKETCHES

SUBJECT.	AUTHOR.	PAGE.
Absent Members	Dr. A. B. Isham	303
Advance and Retreat	Wm. H. Hibbard	250
Andersonville	W. V. Bowles	272
Andersonville	John F. Simpson	288
Appendix		302
Appomattox	Farnham Lyon	65
Appomattox	Andrew Pray	173
Army Traffic	O. H. Perry	135
Attacked by a Woman	W. C. Barden	248
Battle Near Richmond, 1864	A. C. Litchfield	28
Booth, John Wilkes, Watching for	E. O. Russell	184
Brandy Station, Battle of	Geo. G. Briggs	35
Cedar Creek, Battle of	Jas. L. Carpenter	59
Condensed Statistics		VII.
Countermanding Gen. Sheridan's Order	Wm. Hastings	262
Death of a Gallant Officer		159
Disappointments	William O. Lee	284
Experience, An	N. H. Space	237
Flag of Truce, The	Geo. G. Briggs	40
	Frank A. Barr	
Foraging Around Trevilian's Station	James L. Rock	147
Gettysburg, Battle of	G. A. Armstrong	155
Gettysburg, Battle of, "Letter"	J. G. Birney	158
Gettysburg	J. L. Carpenter	56
Granger's Major H. W., Death	David B. Rose	125
Incidents of the Campaign of 1864	R. M. Bellinger	98
Incident in the History of the 7th Mich. Cav.	D. H. Darling	46
Incident, An	William Fisher	256
Incidents	Rev. Chas. P. Nash	71
Inside Rebel Lines and Not Captured	Ray T. Streeter	102
Introductory	Compiler	III.
Kilpatrick's Raid Around Richmond, 1864	D. G. Genney	212

SUBJECT.	AUTHOR.	PAGE.
Kilpatrick's Raid Around Richmond	W. H. Pollard	176
Kilpatrick's Raid Around Richmond	Andrew Pray	171
Lee's Surrender	B. Hulce	264
Left on Picket	E. Von Daniels	143
Lost My Leg, When I	O. A. Jubb	295
Monument, Description of		IX.
Mosby Destroyed Our Train, How	E. R. Havens	90
Mosby's Pickets, Passing	Rev. J. N. Wilson	138
Officers of the Association		I.
Officers, Field and Staff		19
Organization of the 7th Mich. Cav	W. D. Mann	22
Personal Experience on Kilpatrick's Raid	R. H. Holmes	197
Picket Duty, First and Only Two Days	Wm. H. Fisher	86
Picket Line, The	J. Q. A. Sessions	161
Poem, Andersonville	W. V. Bowles	272
Preface		II.
Recollections	Henry DeGraff	78
Recollections, Exciting	Frank Milbourn	182
Reminiscences	H. L. Anthony	97
Reminiscences	E. W. Barnes	269
Reminiscences	Geo. P. Cobb	189
Reminiscences	A. Longman	258
Reminiscences	S. B. Mann	221
Reminiscences	G. W. McCormick	203
Reminiscences	J. L. McDonald	108
Reminiscences	Daniel McNaughton	73
Reminiscences, Mosby's Men	W. W. Raymond	209
Roll of Honor	Dr. A. B. Isham	302
Shenandoah Valley in 1864	W. E. House	117
Sheridan and Custer, Generals, With	Geo. W. Dobson	180
Shock, A	Dr. A. H. Weston	115
Story of the War	J. M. Page	273
Trevilian's Station	W. F. Kenfield	238
Trevilian's Station, Incidents of	Dr. M. A. Shafer	81
Trevilian's Station, Battle of	Harmon Smith	229
Trevilian's Station, Battle of	Robert Sproul	53
Under Command of General Sheridan	Geo. W. Watson	217
Under Fire, The First Time	David Bierd	278
Warrenton Junction, Reconnaissance Around	Wm. G. Gage	129
Washington to Fairfax, Our First March from	O. I. Hunt	105
Winchester	A. Shotwell	167
Yellow Tavern, Death of Major Granger and General J. E. B. Stuart	Dr. A. B. Isham	224